ESSAYS IN RETROSPECT

COLLECTED ARTICLES
AND ADDRESSES

BY

CHAUNCEY BREWSTER TINKER

NEW HAVEN

YALE UNIVERSITY PRESS

LONDON · GEOFFREY CUMBERLEGE · OXFORD UNIVERSITY PRESS

1948

PREFACE

OLD men are supposed to have the privilege, for a reason that I do not pretend to understand, of talking about themselves. This privilege I have used in a somewhat different way by reconsidering thoughts that I have expressed at various times during an unusually long career, and I have here assembled those essays and addresses which I could not bring myself wholly to destroy. They represent some of the chief interests which I have had for many years, poetry, painting, teaching, and, above all, that strange position in which man finds himself in a universe that eludes all comprehension. I now fling them out like the bantling on the rocks, to live or die, in the hope that they may not be without some casual interest to those concerned, like myself, with some of the more significant problems of our little life.

Most of these essays, as their title indicates, have been published before, and are reprinted with such alterations as it was found impossible to resist; but I have not tried to bring them up to date, nor even to make them conform to my opinions as they have changed during the years. Many of these papers are drawn from a quiet repose in the files of highly regarded magazines, where some may think it would have been judicious to leave them undisturbed. They are now revived not "by request of friends," but by kind permission of the editorial boards who first displayed an interest in them. The essays on Shelley, Housman, and Trollope are from The Yale Review; those on The Great Diarist, Sitter and Portrait, and Ancestor-Worship appeared in The Atlantic Monthly. Those on Johnson, the Brontës, the Pre-Raphaelites, and the Courteous Reader *are from* The Saturday Review of Literature. *I have omitted certain passages which seemed to repeat what I had said before, but I can hardly hope to have eliminated them all. I have not thought it necessary to multiply footnotes whose only object was to call attention to the fact that a person referred to had since been knighted or raised to the peerage, or, mayhap, have passed to a reward of a different sort. Furthermore, as these essays are intended for the "gentle reader," I have not thought it necessary to burden them with footnotes regarding sources and dates which would be appropriate in a work of a more strictly scholarly kind.*

November, 1947

CONTENTS

Courteous Reader

"Gentle Reader, I desire no better Patron for this my rusticke Dialogue than thy favourable smile . . . I referre my bold enterprise to thy best censure, and these homely lines to thy most favourable construction."

A Curry-Combe for a Coxe-Combe. 1615.

SOME years ago a lady, who shall here be nameless, protested in a letter to the *Times Literary Supplement* about its reception of her recently published poem. The reviewer of this unusual volume had described the poetess as employing "a gnomic mode of expression" and "a private idiom" which placed the poem beyond the comprehension of the average reader. The author herself had described her work as

A little all that more is
According to the trouble you can take.

The reviewer implied that the number who would take the trouble was not large. At this the poetess took umbrage and protested. The burden of understanding a poet's experience is, she contended, "on the reader"; the author cannot be the "slave" of persons of unknown capacity for response.

The reader is in the position of calling on me, not of being called on by me . . . nor do I hawk my hospitality. I give out indication of my willingness to dispense hospitality on a basis that preserves my integrity as a host. When I say, "I am 'at home,'" I am being sincerely friendly. When criticism replies, "So am I," it is being meanly facetious.

Now all this is highly significant, not because of the wrath of the lady—for poets have been indignant at reviewers ever since they began to practice—but because of the way in which the reader is treated by the author. The hostess declines to make much of him or to woo him with jam and judicious advice. He must not expect the poet to supply him with wits or a "capacity for response."

The time is past when the reader could expect flattery and thanks from the maker of the book, who pretended that he cared for nothing else in life, inasmuch as it was for the gentle reader that the song was sung, and for him that the story was written. Even if the listeners were not many, it was proper for the poet to express a certain gratitude to them, and to boast of having an audience fit though few. But now the reader may half suspect that he is about to be shouldered out of the poetic world altogether. The poets too frequently suggest that they belong to an order apart, that they have decided to write for themselves and let the reader go hang. Their poetry is written to "release the ego," or to satisfy the performer, not the auditor. And so our poetess sits "at home,"

> Like a high-born maiden
> In a palace-tower,

soothing her laden soul by singing to herself. If the wayfarer chooses to go in unto her, he must not expect to be welcomed with anything like gratitude, nor must he interrupt or ask to understand. He must not even pretend to comprehend too much of it all, because it is not for him that the music is sung.

It is the utterance of an intensely vivid consciousness, which may or may not be intelligible to him, but which is "torturing" the unwilling words "to its own likeness." If the reader is incapable of a response, he had better retire quietly from the scene, and buy a detective story. The gods did not make him poetical, and there's an end on't.

Well, it has been thought through the ages that readers were all too prone to retire from the scene, and that such few as betrayed a disposition to remain and listen were worth winning. If a little cajolery would hold them, the poet did not hesitate to employ it. Thus Tasso, in lines finely rendered by the Elizabethan Fairfax:

> Thither, thou know'st the World is best inclin'd
> Where luring *Parnass* most its Sweet imparts,
> And Truth convey'd in Verse of gentle Kind,
> To read perhaps will move the dullest Hearts:
> So We, if Children young diseas'd we find,
> Anoint with Sweets the Vessel's foremost Parts
> > To make them taste the Potions sharp we give;
> > They drink deceiv'd, and so deceiv'd they live.

The dullest, you see, are worth saving; and the poet's function is comparable to that of the physician, who lures the patient to drink—and live.

But these are deserted heights of "Parnass," on which our poetess has no desire to exist. She prefers to remain "at home," receiving her friends. One can but wonder how many guests there are. I remember to have heard the depressing story of a little girl who longed to give a party. All was made ready, sweetmeats prepared, the house decked out for a festive occasion, and the child gaily attired to meet her guests. But nobody came. The little girl was "at home," and there the affair ended.

The notion that an author may preserve his "integrity as a host" is nonsense. A poet, like other writers, solicits a hearing, and the act of solicitation cannot be accomplished without a certain gesture toward the public. Touch print and you will be, in some sense, defiled. For you, privacy and the cool charms of obscurity are gone. You have descended into the market place, and plead to be attended to. Between an orator on a soapbox shouting to the passer-by and a poet shyly proffering a slender volume of verse there is no essential difference in kind. Both would fain be heard.

The Oriental storyteller, surrounded by a group of auditors ready to pay for their entertainment, is one of the enduring examples of poetic activity. Both poet and storyteller have wares for sale, and both of them profess to provide something worthy of attention—entertainment or instruction—something, moreover, that shall presumably be of more value than the hearer's uninterrupted meditations. It is this that the poet has been offering to do ever since the bard in the *Beowulf* struck his lyre (if he had one), and cried "Hwaet!" to attract the attention of his listeners. The whole tradition of literature is in startling contrast to the modern contempt for the public. Hamlet, it may be recalled, knew that some of a dramatist's fine strokes were caviar to the general, but he was not above making verses for a play himself. But when Mr. MacLeish assumes the role of Hamlet today (in his "Hamlet of A. MacLeish"), he expresses a very different attitude to the public. In his bitter musings he comes to feel that to write poetry is to

shout
For hearing in the world's thick dirty ear.

There is, of course, no specific charge against readers today; but the notion seems to be that they are somehow representative of a great unwashed democracy, with mob emotions. They have itching if not dirty ears. At other times they are held to be, for one purpose or another, mid-Victorian, sentimental, conventional, orthodox, lovers of Longfellow and tameness, and (often) college professors.

Now it would seem to be logical, if the poets thus despise their readers, for them to keep silence. And thus, indeed, does the poet just quoted reason with himself:

> O shame, for shame to suffer it, to make
> A skill of harm, a business of despair,
> And like a barking ape, betray us all
> For itch of notice.
> O be still, be still,
> Be dumb, be silent only. Seal your mouth.

Yes, there is a sad and golden dignity about silence, but it lets the whole cause of poetry go by default. A Milton that is mute is a Milton that is inglorious. It is the lot of a poet to break silence, to make a spectacle of himself, to unpack his heart with words, to insist upon telling his grief or his grievance, his joy, disillusion, hope, fear—what not. Poets are under the goad of the muses. It is at once their glory and their shame.

It is often the poets' notion—and it is defensible enough—that the passion they utter is so sacredly intimate and so intensely personal that its criticism by individuals and its commendation by the public are very nearly an impertinence. It is true that in much of the world's finest poetry the note is so poignantly intimate that the reader feels almost as if he had his ear to the confessional screen. Nevertheless, in his most piercing intimacies the poet cannot wholly forget that his art is essentially one of communication, or he will abandon language altogether and utter only inarticulate cries. And inarticulate passion is not poetry, but only its rough material. It is because of this that the poets have so often insisted that the emotion expressed in verse has somehow been altered since it was first experienced. It has suffered a sea change into something rich and strange. It has passed through a crucible, been recollected in tranquillity, become "universalized" so that it is emblematic of the experience of many men, not merely of that of the poet alone.

The modern confusion in the reader's mind is paralleled in the bewildering disorder and rival claims of the poetic world itself. No historian of English poetry can feel any particular confidence as he attempts to record for posterity the state of things today. Schools have, of course, disappeared. It is not likely that poets intent on being as vividly personal as possible will ally themselves with any "movement" or submit to the charge of following and (perhaps) imitating a master. The very thing against which they contend is the authority of schools and movements and masters. But the freedom which they so ardently desire must be bought with a price, and the price is the shifting sand on which all poetic reputations today may be said to repose. Where will all these reputations be a half a century from now?

It is instructive to turn back for a moment and contrast the order and confidence of the late-Victorian world. I select a single and a homely example of what was thought of contemporary English poetry some sixty-five years ago. It was in 1882 that Mr. Kegan Paul put forth an anthology of verse entitled, *Living English Poets*. It was, if I am not mistaken, edited

by the youthful Canon Beeching, and it was furnished with a
frontispiece in black and white drawn by Walter Crane in his
happiest manner. It represented the slopes of Parnassus on
which, in various attitudes, were represented the five chief
poets of England who were still alive and active: Tennyson,
Browning, Arnold, Swinburne, and Morris. The anthology
contained, very properly, examples of the work of minor poets
also: Miss Rossetti, Patmore, Newman, William Barnes, Aus-
tin Dobson, and others. The list was intentionally inclusive,
but none of the names is wholly forgotten or negligible today.
The pleasant little volume represented a community of interests existing among poets, critics, publishers, and readers.
The frontispiece is, however, more significant of the steadiness
of critical opinion in the 'eighties than the contents of the
volume. For Mr. Crane's five poets alive in 1882, are precisely
the five that a historian of English poetry today would select
to represent that world. All five—Tennyson, Browning, Arnold,
Swinburne, Morris—are, in some sense, on Mount Parnassus,
though no critic, naturally enough, would have the same ardor
for any of them that he might well have felt fifty years ago. But
these are the five that he would have to choose as forces to be
reckoned with in nineteenth-century poetry. D. G. Rossetti,
Clough, and Mrs. Browning were all dead before the anthology
appeared, and so do not complicate our case.

Now suppose an artist were confronted today with such a
subject as was assigned to Walter Crane, how would he set
about making a choice? How populate Parnassus today?
Might he not well fear that his choice would be of so highly personal a kind as to displease the purchasers of the book? Might
he not justly fear being ridiculous in the eyes of posterity?
Yeats, AE, Davies, Housman, and Kipling, alas, have gone

from us. Mr. T. S. Eliot must be chosen, for presumably he is in some sense still the leader of the younger group. And then there is the laureate. (Does the laureate still have his partisans?) Ought Mr. Humbert Wolfe to be included? Or Mr. Sassoon? What has become of Mr. Graves? On the horizon are an interesting group, led by Mr. Auden and Mr. Spender. Then there is Miss Sitwell who reads poetry through a megaphone. Is H. D. forgotten? Is Binyon still read? (But we forget, he, too, is no more.) Of course Mr. De la Mare must be prominently placed, and Mr. Blunden and Miss Sackville-West must be considered. And moreover there is Mr. Abercrombie. What a world! It is hardly surprising if the reader's mind spins at the thought of keeping in touch with it all. There is much in it that is admirable and lovely, but where is the critic who shall sift it out for us? And all this leaves out of account the whole realm of American poetry. But that is another story.

There is one last reason for the confusion in the mind of the gentle reader which it is deemed hardly permissible even to state nowadays. One must no longer lament the passing of standards or ask for any agreement among poets respecting fundamental matters such as meter, the nature of beauty, and the end and aim of poetic activity. Yet one cannot help feeling that it would be a good thing for the state of poetry and for the poets, too, if the courteous reader knew what it was all about, and felt that his smile and his "favorable construction" had something to do with its prevalence. It is no defense of the poets to say that our present Babel has been caused by the modern doubt of all ultimate truths, for it is just the office of poets to discover and to teach these very ultimates. If poets are ready to surrender this office to the scientists, then they and their readers are indeed in miserable plight.

That there are still poets alive who feel the necessity of some sort of central and constructive thinking is shown by the development of T. S. Eliot. The author of "The Waste Land" and "Ara Vus Prec" has never been considered timorous or stodgy, or inclined to range himself with the Tories of the literary world. He it was who flung conventions to the scrap heap and made way for the radicals to march in and take possession of the field. And then, because he could not rest with a philosophy of negativism, he made a definite act of allegiance, and announced to friends and critics alike that he had taken a stand. In the preface to his essays, *For Lancelot Andrews* (1928), he explained the exact nature of his allegiance in politics, in literature, and in religion. Great was the fluttering in the dovecote of the minor poets. Followers fell away from him in grief and incredulity. Critics pointed him out with scorn. It may be doubted whether Mr. Eliot will, in our time, quite recover from the evil reputation which he won for himself as a man who knew exactly what he believed; but he had the honor of going straight to the heart of the modern difficulty. He revealed his conviction that spirits must be finely touched ere there can be fine issues, and so, by expressing his conviction that noble poetry can spring only from an august conception of the dignity of human life, he assumed at once a position among the poets of his time as distinguished as it was solitary.

II

The Great Diarist, and Some Others

I REMEMBER to have read somewhere in the pages of Mark Twain the account of a youthful attempt to keep a diary, the result of which was the endless repetition of the sentence, "Got up, washed; went to bed." I forget what the anecdote was meant to illustrate, the fact that the diarist's art is a difficult one, or that there was nothing in a boy's life fit to record. In either case, I am probably wrong, yet I wish to submit modestly but firmly that Mark Twain was mistaken. A true diarist will be interesting about anything, no matter how trivial; whether the dog has ruined the carpet or a king been seated on his ancestral throne, the true journalist is never dull. The Creator has dispensed him from boring his readers.

Take, for instance, the three incidents of the day recited above: one gets up, one washes, and one goes to bed, all events sufficiently common, even washing, to seem useless to the literary artist; yet who would spare them from the pages of Samuel Pepys? "Up and to my office" . . . "Up betimes, and to St. James's" . . . "Lay in bed, it being Lord's Day, all the morning, talking with my wife; then up." I find that I resent the entries in his *Diary* that lack this familiar beginning, as though something essential had been omitted. As for the companion phrase, consecrated to the ending of the day, it has achieved a popularity that bids fair to enshrine it in the daily speech of men, "And so to bed." . . . Sentiment will ultimately make an epitaph of it, like, "Say not good night," or "Good-by, proud world."

As for bathing, that may be the most exciting of events, as the poets know: "the cool silver shock" of the plunge, whether it be into the pool's living water, or into the chilly waters of the domestic tub.

Up, and to the office . . . where busy till noon, and then my wife being busy in going with her woman to a hot-house to bathe herself, after her long being within doors in the dirt, so that she now pretends to a resolution of being hereafter very clean. How long it will hold I can guess.

22nd. Lay last night alone, my wife after her bathinge lying alone in another bed. So cold all night.

25th. Thence home to the office, where dispatched much business; at night, late home, and to clean myself with warm water; my wife will have me, because she do herself, and so to bed.

Verily nothing that is human is alien to the diarist. For him life contains nothing that is common or dull. Let him tell us what he ate for dinner, how cold he was in bed, how a duchess smiled on him, what is his balance at the bank, how he lost his faith in God, or regained it, or had been snubbed by a rival or cursed his enemy in his heart, or cast eyes of desire upon the parlormaid—all is grist to his mill. How near is grandeur to our dust! How easily does this mortal put on immortality.

But immortality is bought at a price, even by the diarist. It is a razor edge, as the Mohammedan might tell us, across which the pilgrim to heaven must make his way. And the diarist, like the rest of us, is in perpetual danger of damnation for his sins. He may make much of them in his journals, and even delight us by his delight in them, but he must not take pride in displaying them. He would do well to set down naught in the hope of admiration or in the fear of derision. Thus, if a genuine diarist records that he was cold in bed, he does so with a childlike simplicity, as a grievance, as a count against his wife, or as a humble fact; but the gods forbid him to enjoy the sensation of being clever at the work. As soon as he becomes clever, amending his style, and aspiring to smart phrase and graceful posture, he is a self-conscious artist, a skillful operative. He may, with luck, become Shaw or Mencken, but he will never be a Samuel Pepys. The artist seeks, properly enough, success and applause; but the diarist is not concerned with such matters. He is not permitted to anticipate or even desire them. When once his record is complete, he may realize, I suppose, in some dim fashion, that he has prevailed over oblivion, so that he cannot destroy his work, even though he may, so far as the outward and surface part of him is concerned, be unwilling that any eye save his own should ever see what he has written.

This setting down of events and emotions precisely as one has known them, and almost immediately after their occurrence, simply, and because one must—this is the *sine qua non* of a true diarist. But why the compulsion? What is the spur that drives him on?

He must, I imagine (for I am myself no diarist), set down an abstract and brief chronicle of life because he loves it so. He cannot bear to let it all perish without leaving a trace behind. I do not mean that he will record only his delights. Sin, pain, and woe have their place in the great diaries of the world, and must always have, since they are of the very fabric of existence. Indeed, a journal may be almost exclusively a recital of these, so as to become painful or even tragic reading; but through it all there must be a conviction on the part of the writer that, in spite of it all, life was worth having. It would not be easy to discover a diarist who was also a sincere and heartbroken pessimist, one who really felt that life was not worth living. If life be not worth living, obviously a journal is not worth keeping.

Consider a diary as unlike that of Pepys as could be found, *La Doulou,* by Alphonse Daudet—*Suffering,* or, as I prefer to render the Provençal word, *Anguish.* It is the intimate and personal account of the daily life of a man suffering from locomotor ataxia. He watches the approach of his enemy day by day and inch by inch, and studies his own physical, nervous, and mental symptoms with the most anxious attention, like a prisoner condemned to the scaffold who counts the moments and days lapsing from him. He knows that he is conquered, but he will not surrender. Like the hero in the old ballad, when he can no longer stand on his feet, he fights upon his knees; he struggles not so much for himself as for his wife and family, in the hope of concealing from them as long as he can the horrible trap into which he has fallen. Thus *La Doulou* has the intimate, secret note which marks this kind of writing; but at no point does Daudet curse life and lie down to die. Dark as are the colors of his book and dire as is its story, there is something invigorating in the account of the victim's prolonged agony, for it represents the triumph of a human soul. The book is a vivid contrast to the diary and letters of Obermann, which, even when they have something cheerful to record, exude a lethal atmosphere which makes the reader, like the author, long to have done, not only with the book, but with the whole futile business of living.

A recent diary is that of the Yorkshire parson, the Reverend Benjamin Newton, a typical sporting clergyman of the early nineteenth century, who was interested in everything about him, except perhaps the souls of his flock. Like Pepys, he was susceptible to the charms of the other sex, and kept a list of handsome women in numerical order according to their beauty of (a) face and (b) figure. He is perpetually entertaining because of his unfailing vivacity. This same quality endears Pepys to his readers:

I home to set my journall for these four days in order, they being four days of as great content and honour and pleasure to me as ever I hope to live or desire, or think any body else can live. For methinks if a man would but reflect upon this, and think that all these things are ordered by God Almighty to make me contented . . . in my life and matter of mirth, methinks it should make one mightily more satisfied in the world than he is.

Neither syntax nor theology here is beyond criticism, but what vitality it reveals, what sincerity, what contentment! I like to think that the gratitude of young Mr. Pepys was acceptable to his Creator:

So dispatched all my business, having assurance of . . . all hearty love from Sir W. Coventry, and so we staid and saw the King and Queene set out toward Salisbury, and after them the Duke and Duchesse, whose hands I did kiss. And it was the first time I did ever, or did see any body else, kiss her hand, and it was a most fine white and fat hand. But it was pretty to see the young pretty ladies dressed like men, in velvet coats, caps with ribbands and with laced bands, just like men. Only the Duchesse herself it did not become. They gone, we with great content took coach again, and hungry come to Clapham about one o'clock, and Creed there too before us, where a good dinner . . . and so to walk up and down in the gardens, mighty pleasant. By and by comes by promise to me Sir G. Carteret, and viewed the house above and below, and sat and drank there, and I had a little opportunity to kiss and spend some time with the ladies above, his daughter, a buxom lass, and his sister Fissant, a serious lady, and a little daughter of hers that begins to sing prettily. Thence with mighty pleasure, with Sir G. Carteret by coach, with great discourse of kindnesse, with him to my Lord Sandwich, and to me also; and I every day see more good by the alliance. Almost at Deptford I 'light and walked over to Half-way House, and so home, in my way being shown my cozen Patience's house, which seems, at distance, a pretty house. At home met the weekly Bill, where above 1,000 encreased in the Bill, and of them in all about 1,700 of the plague, which hath made the officers this day resolve of sitting at Deptford, which puts me to some consideration what to do. Therefore home to think and consider of every thing about it, and without determining anything, eat a little supper, and to bed, full of the pleasure of these 6 or 7 last days.

All this mighty pleasure in the midst of a plague-stricken city! Terror hangs over the world like an ever-blackening cloud, but the diarist's appetite for existence endures undiminished. And so it remains to the end of the journal, when, with the dread of blindness descending upon him and faced with the necessity of closing his diary, he can still record:

Dined at home, and in the afternoon by water to White Hall, calling by the way at Michell's where I have not been many a day till just the other day, and now I met her mother there, and knew her husband to be out of town. And here je did baiser elle, but had not opportunity para hazer some with her as I would have offered if je had had it. And thence had another meeting with the Duke of York, at White Hall, on yesterday's work, and made a good advance; and so, being called by my wife, we to the Park, Mary Batelier and a Dutch gentleman, a friend of hers, being with me. Thence to "The World's End," a drinking-house by the Park; and there merry, and so home late.

No trace here of gloom or apprehension; yet the sentences speed forward to the most pathetic utterances of the great *Diary*. Even as he prays for mercy in the blindness that is coming on him, he does not forget his "amours to Deb" and all "other pleasures" which his eyesight now compels him to resign.

This very quality in which Pepys excels was well described by another great writer of journals: "The minds of some men are like a dark cellar—their knowledge lies concealed; while the minds of others are all sunshine and mirror, and reflect all that they read or hear in a lively manner."

These are the words of James Boswell, a man who, quantitatively at least, rivals Pepys as a diarist. Pepys covers but nine years; Boswell, who had no trouble with his visual organs, remained an inveterate journalist to the end and, no doubt, presented himself at the gate of Heaven, notebook in hand. Now Boswell was a vastly less healthy person than Pepys; he suffered through life from a recurrent melancholia which introduces the strangest lights and shadows into his journals; but in his happier hours he had a very high degree indeed of the passion which I have been describing. Johnson himself called Boswell's fondness for the metropolis a "gust for London." And there are other powers which Pepys and Boswell share.

Both, for instance, were collectors. Both belong to that hungry set who save things, who gather relics and preserve souvenirs, who love long rows of well-filled shelves and all the paraphernalia of a library. These men leave treasures to posterity.

There is an intimate connection between this mania and the

relish for existence which both men display so noticeably. It is because of his gusto that the diarist attempts to preserve some memorial of it, however inadequate. The closer his record to the event itself, the more nearly satisfied he will be. Boswell provides many amusing examples of this desire for verisimilitude. Once when he sent his friend Temple as a sort of ambassador to the young lady with whom he was, or thought he was, in love, he provided him with a long series of detailed directions, the most pointed of which is the command, "Take notes." By taking notes, you see, the ambassador may hope to preserve not only the *ipsissima verba* of the interview but even the very atmosphere and tone of it. The incident will be preserved, as book collectors say, "in the original condition." As long as the scenes of one's past are dear to the heart, so long will a man try to prepare for his future nostalgia by the writing of diaries and the preservation of relics. A true diarist is like a great portrait painter who takes his own likeness. The *Diary* of Mr. Pepys is, in a way, the greatest *Selbstbildnis* ever painted. "A man loves to review his own mind," said Johnson to Mrs. Thrale; "that is the use of a diary or journal." To whom Lord Trimlestown, who was present, said, "True, Sir. As the ladies love to see themselves in a glass, so a man likes to see himself in his journal."

All the reader's interest in the mirror of a mind arises from a belief in the author's truthfulness. Any suspicion of insincerity, any hint that the writer is looking over his shoulder to see whether he is being admired or marveled at, any betrayal of a hope that it will one day get into good black print—this will at once, in some degree, vitiate the reader's pleasure. For the reader of diaries is an eavesdropper. He has his ear to the keyhole, seeking to pry into intimacies. If he suspects that the conversation which he is overhearing is intended for his ear and that the speaker wants to be overheard, all the fun ends at once. Neither the *Soliloquies* of St. Augustine nor the *Confessions* of J. J. Rousseau (different as they are) is a true diary, for both men are too much interested in the reader's response to what has been set down. Miss Burney, too, is aware of her audience and indulges her love of fine writing—a sin of which Pepys was as ignorant as the babe unborn. She sometimes carries her art to the point at which one begins to wonder how much of the original fact is left. She was an inaccurate person, with no special respect for dates. How far does her indifference to such detail extend? To the words alone? Or to whole conversations? Are the speeches she writes down like those of the generals in Thucydides?

But there is no carelessness or inaccuracy, no rhetoric or heightening, in Pepys or Boswell. Both men were professionally concerned with recording facts: Pepys was engaged in filing records for the Naval Office—lists of men o' war, with their tonnage and personnel, their movements and whereabouts, and thousands upon thousands of facts of no special interest to posterity. Boswell, as a Scotch lawyer, had to present his cases to the court in written form. Such work begets in a man a sense of fact and a respect for the moving finger of time. He is not likely to date an important letter "Wednesday."

Much of our pleasure in reading Pepys springs, then, from our conviction of its authenticity. It is this that sweeps us along page after page, over the names of persons of whom we know nothing. But we do feel that they are genuine, like the persons whom we pass in the street, even though we can tell nothing whatever about them. Some of them are acquainted with Pepys, and we are acquainted with him—that is sufficient.

With a few of them, we too become better acquainted as we read on, so that if we persevere we find our pleasure constantly mounting, since our knowledge of what is going on is gradually clarified. We shall never come to a perfect vision of it all; even the most painstaking research will never attain to that, but life as it was three hundred years ago, and Samuel Pepys in his habit as he lived, these we may come to know.

Let us not mistake. Pepys is not great merely because he brings us into contact with the exciting events of his time. True, he lived through the *annus mirabilis,* 1666, and so had personal knowledge of the defeat of the Dutch fleet, the great plague that swept over the city, and the Great Fire which swept over it in a more literal sense. These are important events, as are a thousand others with which Pepys brings us in contact, and so the *Diary* is an invaluable sourcebook for historians; but this is not the reason that Pepys has the devotion of his readers.

The fact is that the man had the fine art of making his record sparkle with vitality. I cannot analyze that gift. I have never met anybody who could. Most essayists on Pepys—and there are many delightful ones—rely for their charm on liberal quotations from the *Diary.* The more quotations, the more charm. The essayist usually contents himself, as in the present instance, with a characterization of the man, not with an analysis of his style. How shall one show the component parts of anything so artless?

Yet Pepys was an artist, and I believe that he knew it. It would be more accurate to say that he must in time have come to know it. It seems to me preposterous to try to believe that a man who has produced a vast work of genius should be unaware of what he has done. He may very well have been ignorant of its largest relations and of its permanent value to mankind; but that he should have had no intimation of its pictorial and panoramic quality, no realization of the fact that it plumbs the depths of human nature—this is beyond belief. I should as soon expect the builder of the pyramids to be unaware of the shape which he had erected.

And I believe, furthermore, that it was this knowledge of what he had done that prevented Pepys from destroying or ordering the destruction of the *Diary*. He could not do it, nor do I think that another man who had created such a thing (if we may tolerate such an assumption) could bring himself to destroy it. For Pepys it would have been a kind of suicide.

He was aware of course that it could be readily decoded —was not the same code used in his office?—and indeed a cipher that cannot be decoded would be simply another form of oblivion. And yet there was a certain protection in it. A cipher does furnish a screen against casual observation; a long diary, like that of Pepys, might hope to survive many years unread. After a lapse of a couple of generations, secrecy was no longer of consequence. This was perhaps, consciously or subconsciously, what Pepys wanted. He wanted privacy—protection, that is, from inquisitiveness and the derision of his familiars, and this the cipher afforded, and would probably continue to afford as long as any of his contemporaries existed. To most of us posterity hardly matters. The genial soul of Pepys may very well have been content to meet it and entrust his reputation to it. I cannot see why any man should shrink from that. It is one's neighbors and one's relatives whom one wishes to elude. In the masquerade of life a man does not care to give himself away. It is a world in which we are all making a plucky pretense. One takes conscious pride in "getting away" with one's pose, and none more so than Pepys in public life. But there is a solid comfort in making a clean breast of it, whether one is purging the stuffed bosom of the perilous stuff that weighs upon the heart or merely setting down the various devices by which he has succeeded in snatching the pleasures of existence as they fly. But it is so hard to get a hearing and to utter all that one would like to say! Confessors, I have been told, find some difficulty in persuading their penitents to abridge the tale of their sins. "No excuses, please. No details," they must be always hinting. But the diarist feels no such restraint, and hears no such monitor. He may go on forever.

And as for being read by posterity, is there not a certain pleasure in that, even though everything has to come out? It is certainly no worse than dying and meeting the recording angel, which is an experience that awaits us all. But thanks be to God, it is an angel, and not our neighbors, our wives, or our professors whom we have to meet. Perhaps it will not be so bad after all. Who knows but there may be a solid satisfaction in it, upon getting a hearing at last? The angel will probably do the best he can for us. It is the way of angels.

Posterity has been friendly to Pepys. Not even an angel, I imagine, could have been more indulgently kind. Where is there an author more beloved by his readers? Boswell is still despised by multitudes, Walpole is occasionally disliked, Cowper pitied, and Rousseau distrusted. But Pepys is like Lamb, loved by everybody. I have encountered but one sneer at Pepys, and that was from the pen of a communist writing for the *New Masses,* comrade Michael Gold: "Samuel Pepys is esteemed by bourgeois readers because he did the things they do, or want to do: he accepted bribes, he dodged his taxes, he was unfaithful . . . to his wife, he beat his servants." Well, in the new world of communism we are, I suppose, to look for none of these dreadful things, for sin (and the knowledge of it) will have been abolished (by law), and nobody will care whether he is loved by posterity or not.

III

Samuel Johnson

I. LITERARY MONARCH

IT has long been customary for historians and critics of English literature to assert that in the mid-eighteenth century Samuel Johnson "occupied the throne of letters," and reigned over the literary world as Ben Jonson, Dryden, and Pope had done before him. He is represented as having created reputations by a word or a nod. "The fierce light," said Mr. Seccombe, "that plays upon the throne of an elected monarch was henceforth [from 1764] upon Johnson." Others accepting this view often added that Johnson was the *last* of such kings. It is Macaulay, however, who gives us the most detailed account of this dictatorship. It operated chiefly, it appears, through the Literary Club, and the power of the dictator and his group was so formidable that "verdicts" on new books "were speedily known over all London, and were sufficient to sell off a whole edition in a day or to condemn the sheets to the service of the trunk-maker or the pastry-cook."

Kingship in any of its eighteenth-century phases is but a mournful study, and Johnson's royal authority in the literary world is not even a happy exception to the rule. The age in which he lived was no more inclined to acknowledge the authority of a literary than of a political monarch. The louder their "king" might be in promulgating a view or in assigning an author his proper rank in the literary world, the more dis-

posed was the public to question the legality of his pronouncements. Johnson had, in truth, the royal manner—a fact that
tends to keep alive the tradition of his kingship—but his actual
authority, when it is critically examined, is seen to have been
shadowy enough. It is said, for example, that he could confer
or withhold literary repute. Yet he would have been glad to
lower the contemporary esteem for Fielding and for Sterne. He
proclaimed loudly enough that Harry Fielding was a "barren
rascal" who knew only the shell of life and who, as a novelist,
was inferior to Fanny Burney. He detested "the man Sterne,"
and was rash enough to say of *Tristram Shandy,* which has
been a delightful and popular book in every age, that it "did
not last." But despite such *dicta,* the reputation of these novelists
continued to rise. On the other hand, he would have been
glad to confer fame as a poet on Isaac Watts, whom he praised
for a vigorous and active imagination, a well-tuned ear, and
an elegant and copious style; but he got laughed at for including
the good Doctor in the collection of the English Poets. He
would have been glad to reduce the reputation of Thomas Gray,
the most popular poet since Pope, of whom with rare infelicity
he remarked, "We have had enough of Gray." He considered
that Goldsmith's *Vicar of Wakefield,* the manuscript of which
he had himself sold to the printers, owed its reputation largely
to the author's *Traveller,* a poem which he always held to be
superior to *The Deserted Village.* His favoritism was notorious,
and was resented quite as bitterly as the favoritism of any other
monarch. He included in his *Lives of the Poets* his biography
of Richard Savage because he had been personally acquainted
with and sorry for that hack writer, whose reputation to this
day reposes largely on this arbitrary inclusion. He praised the
work of Edmund Smith because he had himself spent many

"cheerful and instructive hours at his table." Of a slightly different kind was his treatment of that graceful and delicate poet, William Collins. His sad life was duly recorded by the biographer, but his chiseled and Parian verses were dismissed in a slender paragraph at the end which barely concealed the critic's indifference.

Such ineptitudes did not pass unnoticed by the public. The singular inclusiveness of the collection of the English poets was the subject of special stricture, for not only had Johnson written the life of every "dunce" whom the booksellers had selected, such as Sprat, Duke, and Granville, but by his own effort secured the inclusion of Blackmore, Watts, Pomfret, and Yalden. The voice of derision was raised. Horace Walpole wrote to friends about the book in his most caustic vein. Potter, in his *Enquiry into Some Passages in Dr. Johnson's Lives of the Poets,* quotes some verses which set forth the public attitude to that work:

> Such is the critic who, with wayward pride,
> To Blackmore gives the praise to Pope denied,
> Wakes Yalden's embers, joys in Pomfret's lay,
> But sickens at the heaven-strung lyre of Gray.

As it was with his contemporaries, so it was with his predecessors. He spoke with authority but recognized none. For the universal critical opinion, for that traditional view of English literature, which transcends all merely personal opinion, and which was already full-formed, he showed no particular respect. Swift, he said, had a higher reputation than he deserved. Addison he ranked somewhat below Dr. Arbuthnot, whom he considered as the "first" among the writers of Queen Anne's reign, and the "most universal genius" of that period. His grudging estimate of Milton, who wrote "such poor sonnets," was widely resented in an age which had already returned to Milton. He queried whether Shakespeare often achieved the sublime without being bombastic, and charged him with indulging in quibbles to the sacrifice of "reason, propriety and truth."

When Johnson indulged in the detailed and verbal criticism of particular passages, he was seldom more felicitous than in his general pronouncements. His method consists largely in testing the diction of poetry by common sense. Thus he disposes of one of Gray's most famous odes in a few hasty phrases:

The "Prospect of Eton College" suggests nothing to Gray which every beholder does not equally think and feel. His supplication to Father Thames to tell him who drives the hoop or tosses the ball is useless and puerile. Father Thames has no better means of knowing than himself. His epithet *buxom health* is not elegant; he seems not to understand the word. Gray thought his language more poetical as it was remote from common use.

This is all that Johnson has to say about this poem, though its lapse from sense, if lapse it be, is but a trifling slip in the middle of an ode a hundred lines long. What poem cannot be demolished by a treatment so arbitrary?

"A broken metaphor," as Johnson called it, elicited his harshest censure. He admired Addison's *Letter from Italy,* which, he asserted, had "always been praised, but never praised beyond its merit"; yet he chose one passage to riddle with grapeshot because of a mixed metaphor:

Fir'd with that name,
I bridle in my struggling Muse with pain,
That longs to launch into a nobler strain.

This passage is bad indeed, but so also is Johnson's criticism of it: "To *bridle* a *goddess* is no very delicate idea; but why must she be *bridled?* because she *longs to launch;* an act which was never hindered by a *bridle:* and whither will she *launch?* into a *nobler strain.* She is in the first line a *horse,* in the second a *boat;* and the care of the poet is to keep his *horse* or his *boat* from *singing.*"

Let the candid reader consider how some of the most ecstatic strains in English poetry would fare under the rapid fire of such an attack. Could the poet escape scot free who

> Heard a mermaid on a dolphin's back,
> Uttering such dulcet and harmonious breath
> That the rude sea grew civil at her song,
> And certain stars shot madly from their spheres
> To hear the sea-maid's music?

What would be left of one of the famous passages in a nineteenth-century ode if we took from it every detail inconsistent with common sense?

> Thou wast not born for death, immortal bird,
>   No hungry generations tread thee down;
> The voice I hear this passing night was heard
>   In ancient days by emperor and clown.

Is the value of such a passage to be tested by inquiries concerning the longevity of nightingales?

It would be merely churlish to multiply illustrations of such regrettable opinions as have been cited. It has been important to enumerate them in order to see how our "king" in true royal fashion seems at times to have been fretful and ungenerous. His famous "authority," of which critics have said so much, may seem to be melting away into the caprice of a tyrant whose violence is applauded because it is picturesque and stirring, but whose power to enforce his will is laughed at.

But such a view by no means embraces the full truth. To belittle Johnson as a critic of literature would be to outrage justice and to have done with common sense. He is not only a great critic, but he is one of the few who can be read with continuous delight; one whose opinion is always significant, even when it is not acceptable, and one who can always be read with profit even when we dissent from the view set forth.

The explanation of this singular state of things lies, I think, in the fact that Johnson's criticism is not a *system,* every detail of which must be consistent with certain principles from which all casual expressions are supposed to derive. His words, in truth, have a dogmatic air. He asserts his opinions magisterially. But, though we still read the *Lives of the Poets,* we do not do so to find out what to think about Milton and Pope, but rather to enjoy the humor and the humors, the audacities and the prejudices of a man of genius, who even in his aberrations is always amusing and always stimulating. These, the true Johnsonian has always felt, are more valuable than any system; and even when we concede, as concede we must, that there are frequently at work in his mind great fundamental convictions which are at the very heart and center of the man; still it is an expression of principle which is being ever agitated and deflected, and at times altogether overset by a personality which eludes classification and definition. It is Johnson's *tastes* that we are eager to come at, his feelings about a given work of art and not that "pomp of system and severity of science" (to use a phrase of his own) which he could bring to its praise or its destruction. His preface to Shakespeare, for example, is still delightful reading. Why? Not, surely, because of its finality. Johnson, for all the praise which he mingled with his sanity, spoke no definitive word about Shakespeare. Yet it is a stimulating and useful essay despite its faults; for faults it has. In the whole preface there are not half a dozen quotations from the plays—a count, indeed, would probably reveal that most of the quotations which are used come from Latin sources—and there are not half a dozen references to specific plays or individual characters. Certain conclusions set down by the essayist seem, at first blush, remarkable chiefly for their oddity. Thus Johnson considered the comedies superior to the tragedies since the former spring out of the author's instincts and the latter merely from his skill. He considered that the passion of love had but "little operation" in the plays. These are opinions for which we may feel it would be difficult to give adequate reasons; yet they are interesting and provocative of thought, and that is the function of an essayist. Our pleasure in reading them is not in their perfect justice (as in reading Sainte-Beuve) nor in their swift epigrammatic force (as in reading Hazlitt), but in the stimulus to thought that issues from them. They pique our pride, make us review the evidence, restate the case, and criticize the critic. They certainly do not terminate the discussion but initiate a critical inquiry in us, the readers. It is not that we feel that so preposterous an opinion must be swept aside and our own set up in its place, but rather that so vivid a hypothesis has been struck out that we cannot but take it into account. Such, I think, is the common experience of readers of Johnson. His critical utterances are suggestive, sensible, maddening, humorous, what you will, but they never terminate in the scientific formality of a critique. The most notable example of this is his conversation. He flung out assertions as if to see how they would fare, sink or swim. They were—what else is criticism?—approximations to the truth, a trial flight, a hypothesis, a guess masquerading in dogma. If he convinced his hearers, or frightened them into acquiescence, well and good—that was their concern. If, on the other hand, they picked up the gauntlet, why then, as Rosalind put it, "there begins new matter." *The hunt is up.* And so, "We have had enough of Gray," shouts Johnson, as though awaiting the appearance of a defender. He might of course have introduced the discussion otherwise and perhaps more politely by inquiring, "If I were to assert that we have had enough of Gray, what sort of rebuttal could be made?"

Thus we may conceive of Johnson, not as a judge delivering sentence from the bench, for the existence of a judge implies also that of a jury that has sat upon the cause, but rather as a champion clothed with convictions as with armor, having the sword of wit in his hand, ready to do combat with any comer, and feeling his humanity tingling in every inch of him.

Nor is this an argument for that romantic and belated type of criticism known as "impressionism." Johnson had more to express than mere likes and dislikes. To conceive of his opinions as casual is to forget his scholarship and his long experience with literature as a force in men's lives. Of the truth of this there exists an admirable proof in his treatment of Addison's prose. It seems that he got but little personal pleasure out of it. "He did never like," says Mrs. Piozzi, "although he always thought fit to praise it." Naturally. A man may esteem as invaluable those things which do not always appeal to his personal tastes or his transient needs. So, though he may not have "liked" Addison's prose, Johnson gives us the perfect estimate of it, and later judgments on the same subject read like a quotation:

His prose is the model of the middle style; on grave subjects not formal, on light occasions not grovelling; pure without scrupulosity, and exact without apparent elaboration; always equable, and always easy, without glowing words or pointed sentences. Addison never deviates from his track to snatch a grace; he seeks no ambitious ornaments and tries no hazardous innovations. His page is always luminous, but never blazes in unexpected splendour.

If we listen with reverence to Johnson as he speaks of literature, it is because we feel behind his words, even in their violence and occasional waywardness, a large humanity and a long knowledge against the background of which his views project themselves in sharp relief. His position in the world of letters, even if we demur to its being a king's, was as felicitous and as venerable as a critic's is ever likely to be. When, in 1777, he undertook to prepare for the London publishers what proved in effect to be a biographical and critical history of English poetry from Milton to Gray, he brought to the task an unrivaled knowledge of the facts with which he was to deal. With some of the poets he had come into personal relations. He remembered Pope. He remembered the successive appearance of the poems that made up Thomson's *Seasons*. He remembered the appearance of *Gulliver's Travels,* of *The Castle of Indolence,* of Gay's *Fables* and *Beggar's Opera,* and of Young's *Night-Thoughts,* besides a chaos of lesser works which had to be judged or at least mentioned. And all these he remembered as a man professionally interested in poetry and vitally concerned with its reception. He was himself a poet of no mean rank. In that earlier and silent period of his life he had also seen men who remembered Dryden, and to whom Milton was something more than a famous name. Thus even his prejudices had a venerable history and preserved views and attitudes out of the distant past. All this was much; but it was not Johnson's chief distinction. He had survived to old age and had been able, thanks to the bell-like soundness of his mind, to compare the vivid first impressions of his youth with the calmer views of posterity. He had the priceless privilege of reconsidering his opinions, not once but repeatedly, and of expressing them at last in the fullness of his years and his wisdom.

It would be a delightful task to collect all the personal reminiscences in the *Lives of the Poets,* all the firsthand information, and all the anecdotes that appear there for the first time. A single example serves to illustrate the authenticity which Johnson could lend to his historical writing: "I have heard Mr. Richardson relate that he attended his father the painter on a visit when one of Cibber's pamphlets came into the hands of Pope, who said: 'These things are my diversion.' They sat by him while he perused it and saw his features writhen with anguish." Here, as an illustration of Pope's sensitiveness, is an authenticity of portraiture which is possible only to a poet's contemporaries or to his immediate successors. It is more than gossip, for it reveals that extreme susceptibility which produced much that was best and much that was unworthy in the work of Pope. But it is not such passages as this which constitute the decisive value of Johnson's criticism. If we wish to estimate the extent of his powers, we must set such a passage side by side with one of a very different caliber.

It is the perspective, the proportion, the background of Johnson's remarks that disclose the operation of a mind through a long course of years in which the treasury of experience has been filled. What young man could write such a passage as this?

Good sense alone is a sedate and quiescent quality, which manages its possessions well, but does not increase them; it collects few materials for its own operations and preserves safety, but never gains supremacy. Pope had likewise genius; a mind active, ambitious and adventurous, always investigating, always aspiring; in its widest searches still longing to go forward, in its highest flights still wishing to be higher; always imagining something greater than it knows, always endeavouring more than it can do.

The two passages together illustrate the remarkable union of qualities found in the critical writing of Samuel Johnson at his best: the wealth of information, derived, as it were, from another world in which the author had lived, yet mingling with the wisdom of one looking backward from afar. The whole is set forth with the vigor and the occasional humor and violence of a man who, in his age, has lost nothing of the audacity of youth; one who has done with timid reserve, and, after long reflection is willing to speak out the views that are in him without apology or mincing deference to a public opinion in which he has no faith. Such was the voice of Samuel Johnson in the last decade of his life, and if we do not always defer to it as of royal authority, it is because we find in it a boldness, an acumen, and a suggestiveness worthy of a professional man of letters and of more enduring value to men than the dictates of a king.

II. THE UNACCOUNTABLE COMPANION

THAT a man of such obvious faults as Johnson's should prove to have so enduring a fascination for mankind is a thing to give us pause. Over a hundred years have elapsed since Macaulay drew attention to this phenomenon; yet there has been no dwindling in Johnson's bulky and impressive figure as it recedes into the mists of the past. Why is this? Of late there has been a tendency to regard Johnson as being somehow the symbol and exponent of his age, and he has been said to unite in himself the typical traits of the Englishman. But this view will not bear examination. Carlyle pointed out in 1840 that Johnson who "worshipped in the age of Voltaire" was certainly not typical of his century (that "age of Beelzebub"). And such Christian faith is no less unique than his stalwart opposition to the advance of democracy which was as certainly typical of the period.

If we look critically into such assertions we shall have difficulty in persuading ourselves that Johnson was in any sense whatever a "typical Englishman," if such a being may be said to exist. An Englishman is usually supposed to have a power (highly prized by himself and assiduously cultivated) of self-possession which ignores the possibility of ridicule or the need of correction. But though Johnson despised "foreigners"—those not born east of the Severn and south of the Tweed—he had no skill whatever in the fine art of self-control. He surrendered readily to every fleeting prejudice; he expressed with picturesque extravagance emotions which he regretted half an hour later; he never hid his affection for his friends, his dependents, his black servant, his dead wife, his college, or his cats. He apparently did not fear the charge of sentimentality, the Englishman's bugaboo. He begged the indulgent sympathy and prayers of all who came into close contact with him. Is this, one asks, "typically English"? If so we must revise our estimate of that remarkable people.

Nor is there any evidence that Johnson had the typical English love of sport, that one passion of the Englishman which is wholly unrepressed. For though Johnson was perhaps "athletic" in a spasmodic fashion, running races barefoot, swinging on gates, climbing trees, and rolling down hill, there is no hint of any regular attention to "exercise" or even to life in the open air. There is, so far as I know, no evidence that Johnson ever went afishing; and though he boasted that he could ride to hounds "as hard as anyone," there is no proof that he often did so. He was not regularly seen at boxing matches or racecourses.

Johnson described himself as a retired and uncourtly scholar, and such indeed he was, and one with no remarkable breadth of interests. To music and to the plastic arts he was in general indifferent, though he could rouse himself to write a preface to Sir Joshua's *Discourses* or Dr. Burney's *History of Music*. Politics bored him, save when he gave himself to the writing of such (perhaps regrettable) pamphlets as *The False Alarm* and *Taxation No Tyranny*. Even the reading of history, but in particular conversation *about* history, bored him. When the conversation turned on the Punic Wars, he "divorced his mind and thought about Tom Thumb." But to poetry and to religion, to the failings and the fortunes of his friends he was never indifferent.

Upon the ordinary routine and the chaotic confusion of life, Johnson brought to play a continuous stream of ideas. He drew the casual affairs of the day and the ordinary topics of conversation into a perspective in which new lights and shadows were suddenly revealed. He lent to the humdrum of life a novelty that was sometimes splendid and sometimes terrifying, but which was always forceful and provocative even when it was unreasonable. To speak in medical terms, he was the great irritant of his circle. Yet in his power there is nothing that is aloof or that is saintly, for he clearly belongs to the same world as do we ourselves. He, too, is doomed to struggle with disease and disappointment, ever conscious of the lost opportunity and the unfulfilled task, with a loving heart which he was forever disgracing by outbursts of spleen and bigotry, with a mind conscious of heroic powers, yet a prey to melancholy and to a fitful purpose;—in a word, a genius, yet a fretful, sinful, and hungry creature like ourselves. Such is the enduring fascination of the man.

IV

Joel Barlow's
Vision of Columbus

CONNECTICUT, I am confident, is the only state in the union that ever produced two epic poets at once. They were Timothy Dwight and Joel Barlow, young men who had lived through the American Revolution and had come out of college filled with ambition for the newborn nation. Why should not America like Greece and Rome have an epic poem? The former of these young aspirants therefore wrote a long poem about Moses, Joshua, and the entry of the Israelites into the Promised Land, and called it *The Conquest of Canaan;* and the other, Barlow, wrote a long reflective poem, *The Vision of Columbus,* printed at Hartford in 1787, the title of which was, many years later, altered to the *Columbiad,* by which name it is known today to the few who remember poems more remarkable for their noble plan and admirable intention than for their successful execution. Neither of our epic aspirants was a poet in any but the loosest sense; yet both of them served the muse and their country in a very definite and perhaps not unworthy way.

Barlow's epic which, in its first form was in nine books, may well have been begun or at least projected, while its author was an undergraduate in Yale College during the Revolutionary War. We know from his own testimony that the whole

poem, save a portion of the seventh book, was composed before
the termination of that war. But even if we had no such information about it, we should easily identify the poem as a
work of the author's early years, for nothing ever glowed more
ardently with the emotions and illusions of youth. The juvenile
poet is consumed with pride in America and in her destiny
among the nations. There is no doubt in his confident young
heart that the political future of the nation will be as splendid
as the mountain chains and expansive lakes that lend majesty
to her landscape. He believes that, under the leadership of
America, the human race will move on from glory to glory.
Commerce is destined to bring about the brotherhood of man
and the equal distribution of the world's wealth. All nations,
kindreds, and tribes will be molded into one great family, with
a universal language and a universal conviction that the needs
and aims of the component nations may all be reconciled by a
central parliament, meeting apparently in Asia Minor, and in
a vast palace where are to deliberate the federated peoples of
the world. (Barlow, thou shouldst be living at this hour.) He
has, or rather Columbus has, a vision of the place, and it is
the crowning and final blessing bestowed upon him:

> Clothed majestic in the robes of state,
> Moved by one voice, in general council meet
> The fathers of all empires: 'twas the place
> Near the first footsteps of the human race . . .
> In this mid region, this delightful clime,
> Rear'd by whole realms, to brave the wrecks of time,
> A spacious structure rose, sublimely great,
> The last resort, the unchanging scene of state . . .
> Hither the delegated sires ascend,
> And all the cares of every clime attend.

But there are earlier visions revealed to Columbus. He is shown the whole panorama of American history (with excursions into Chile and Peru). He is shown General Washington in his early and in his later career as a soldier. He is present at the battle of Bunker Hill and sees in vast epic procession—for is there not always room for such matters in epic narrative?—the great leaders of America. Much of this recalls the lists of ships and peoples in the *Iliad* and the Mount of Vision at the close of *Paradise Lost*. It is pleasant to be able to record in passing that when the poem was announced for publication, General Washington put his name down for twenty copies, and the Marquis de Lafayette for ten. With their fine generosity and interest in the arts to be practiced in the New World, there may have mingled a very natural desire to see what role would be assigned to them in the American epic.

There are two defects in *The Vision of Columbus* which, to mention no others, must forever prevent it from being reckoned a poem. In the first place, the author's style is quite without passion or distinction of any kind. So far as epigram or beauty is concerned, the following couplet is about as good as any that Barlow can write, and, indeed, quite above his average:

> But who can tell the dewdrops of the morn
> Or count the rays that in the diamond burn?

In the second place his epic is without a hero—"an uncommon want," as Byron asserted—since Columbus has nothing whatever to do. He only gazes upon visions called up before him; and as these extend over centuries and over whole continents (seen in bird's-eye) the epic is inevitably without any unity of subject.

It is well to admit all this, for nothing is gained by claiming for a poet qualities that he cannot be shown to possess. But there are features of *The Vision of Columbus* on which we may dwell with pleasure. In 1807, nearly a quarter of a century after its composition in its original form, the poem was revised, expanded, and (rashly, I think) renamed *The Columbiad*. At that time Barlow announced that it was to be regarded as a political poem, designed to encourage republican principles and pride of country. He, perhaps wisely, suppressed the original dedication to King Louis XVI. Such action is judicious and middle-aged, but it lacks something of the boyish spontaneity of *The Vision*. I may smile at the lines,

> The epic Muse sublime
> Hails her new empire on the western clime,

but I like their enthusiasm. I grow somewhat weary of sophisticated young men who have laid aside patriotism with their marbles and their hoops. I am pleased with a young man who felt in all sincerity that his country should and could become eminent in the arts as well as in commerce. I can even be pleased with a young man who believed that our feet were set in a blessed path, a path leading through material progress to a goal and a celestial city. The young Barlow actually believed that the world of 1787 was nearer to the millennium than it had ever been before, and that it was the peculiar privilege of America to lead mankind toward that consummation. A great poet once entitled a volume of verse dealing with poems of a political stripe, *Songs before Sunrise*. Barlow's *Vision* might well have been entitled the *Epic of the Dawning Day;* for in the eighth book the poet concerns himself with the progress of civilization and the poem becomes a kind of *Essay on Man,* his nature and his destiny, now and in future.

There are passages in the epic which startle one by the familiar things or scenes which they mention, even while they make us smile at the incongruous part assigned to them among the nation's young glories. Our colleges, for example. The "seats of science" exist to "nurse the arts and point the paths of fame." So far, so good. But what is this?

> Great without pomp the modest mansions rise:
> Harvard and Yale and Princeton greet the skies.

And then there is Philadelphia, whose walls and pavements sparkle to the sun, and where "the crossing streets in fair proportion run." Independence Hall does not pass unnoticed and neither Penn nor Franklin is forgotten. Indeed, Franklin's lightning rod is, perhaps for the only time, made the subject of descriptive verse.* Franklin has taught the children of Columbus to ward off the "bolts of Fate":

> The pointed steel o'ertops the ascending spire,
> And leads o'er trembling walls the harmless fire.
> In his glad fame while distant worlds rejoice,
> Far as the lightnings shine or thunders raise their voice.

In one respect Barlow's judgment was quite right. He spoke with pride of the American painters, Benjamin West, Copley, Stuart, and John Trumbull, who, for genius, may fairly be associated with their European contemporaries. It is not strange that he thought his friends Dwight and Trumbull destined similarly to excel in the poetic art. In this he happened to be wrong, but the very illusion has something splendid about it, and again I am pleased with a young man who wishes his country to excel in such ways.

* I do not reckon *Eripuit caelo fulmen* as an account of the lightning rod.

In certain very important respects Barlow's sentiments were not only admirable but everlastingly right. He could see no reason why a poet should not flourish in America and find material for poetry all about him. He thought that American poetry should be American and not a feeble reflection of classical or English models. He could see no reason why recent events and familiar scenes should not be used by poets. He speaks freely of the cotton plant and the cornfield.

> The rich pimento scents the neighboring skies,
> And woolly clusters o'er the cotton rise.

Even

> Tobago's plant its leaf expanding yields.

It was not his lot, by his own example, to make these familiar things and familiar scenes glorious in poetry; but he was right in thinking that it might be done. Why should not the Housatonic and the Connecticut rivers be as instinct with poetry as the Tiber and the Thames?

In the ardor of his passionate youth, Joel Barlow believed that the nation which he had just seen come to glorious birth was no less grateful to the poetic aspirant than Greece or Rome; and in such verse as he was capable of producing he set forth this view. The attempt, if not the result, endears him to us. If we as a people have failed to realize the high destiny that he foresaw for us, the fault is ours, not Barlow's, whose conception of the function of poetry was as sound as it was noble.

Shelley Once More

IN his early days of novel writing, when Mr. H. G. Wells was content not only to instruct but to entertain his readers, he published a story entitled *The Wonderful Visit*. It was, if I recall it accurately, the tale of an English clergyman, who, while out gunning for birds in the woods, had the luck to shoot and bring down not a bird but an angel. The creature proved to be a seraph who had winged his way too near the earth and so come within range of the clerical gun. The story that follows recounts the adventures of the angel in this workaday world of ours, until, defeated by the insistent conventions of society, his wings gradually shrink and at last disappear altogether; so that the net result is that there is one more human being (and of human beings there are plenty in the world), and one less seraph (a species in which we are noticeably deficient).

Many, as they read Mr. Wells's fairy tale, were reminded of the poet Shelley. Critics had repeatedly compared him to an angel—a creature from another sphere who had, as it were, lost his way, and somehow become involved in the confusion and trivialities of an alien world and an alien society which he could neither comprehend nor alter, despite convulsive and renewed efforts to do so. This angelic simile has been used so often that it is in danger of getting shopworn, yet nobody who writes about Shelley can succeed in ignoring it. Matthew Arnold's famous dictum about the "beautiful and ineffectual angel, beating in the void his luminous wings in vain," would alone have kept it current. Arnold was, in truth, so pleased with his phrase that, though it was not quite original with him, he repeated it more than once with his customary gusto. Now we must not pause to inquire—as many have already done with no particular result—just what "effectual" activity may reasonably be demanded of an angel, a denizen of another sphere. He could hardly be usefully employed on committees to solicit subscriptions for charitable organizations and increase the size of the community chest. Even if he made himself over into a kind of Poor Richard, could he be depended upon not to disconcert us by suddenly displaying a luminous wing and so reminding us of another kind of existence to which practical people give no thought at all? Perhaps it would be more profitable for us to be content with the unearthly beauty of our celestial visitor, and to tempt him by any means in our power to sing to us of that other world from which he is exiled, and for which he presumably longs as does the moth for the star.

If we have no use for such imponderable results as music but insist, as we are prone to do with the nonconformist, that our visitor shall adopt our own ways, and, furling his wings, don our dress and our busy aims, we shall presently discover that the wonderful guest has gradually turned into a kind of being whom we can neither admire nor love: a *tertium quid,* neither seraph nor honest John Doe, but a flaming rebel. He will curse our way of doing things, initiate foolish reforms, pull down our sacred institutions, lead revolts, and start new and crackbrained ways of conducting the world for us. We shall ere long find it convenient and, indeed, the only sane solution of our difficulties to put the soiled seraph to death and be rid of him for good. Persons should be warned not to bring down such creatures from the heavens. Angels are a nuisance. If they cannot learn to know their place and leave practical, everyday, commonplace men and women alone, they must be put quietly and "effectually" out of the way. A few poets and eccentrics may weep to think that there will be no more flaming odes or shrill war songs from the glorious rebel, but song is easily dispensed with. Anyhow, the world can go about its business as usual.

Now, Percy Bysshe Shelley did not live long enough to get himself put to death by an indignant world, but it is easy enough to imagine such a fate overtaking him in middle age (had he attained to it), for he was often in conflict with the legal authorities by promoting crazy schemes to make things or persons or society different or better or happier. Was he not the victim of hallucinations? Did he not involve himself, in spite of resources that should have been more than adequate, in financial obligations from which he could not extricate himself? And did he not run away from his debts and from officers of the law whose duty it was to see that he did not escape? Did he not detach himself from one wife in order to ally himself with another, and then have the assurance to invite his first consort to come and live with him and the second? Did he not repeatedly and in no uncertain tones describe the incestuous relations of brother and sister? Men have been put out of the way for lesser offenses than these.

Is it not, perhaps, regrettable that we know so much about Shelley's life? Long ago Professor Beers, one of the calmest of critics, remarked, "No one cares anything about his 'philosophy,' and if the details of his futile, unhappy career could be forgotten, it would be better for his memory." And the new biography, in two immense volumes, by Professor Newman White, in spite of its great excellence, hardly alters this view.

There was no intimate, full-length biography of the poet by a contemporary—by one, that is, who, living in daily intercourse with him, "saw Shelley plain." Of the poet in his habit as he lived we can have only broken lights. But there are documents and dates and letters and reminiscences aplenty, and to these Mr. White has given a lifetime of scholarly inspection, and from them he has woven a consistent and at times a thrilling account of a life never lacking in color or in excitement, a career that now trenches on comedy, and now darkens into tragedy. Mr. White has steered his bark with skill between the whirlpool and the threatening rocks. He has, on the one hand, declined to sink his biography into a mere melodramatic novel, and, on the other hand, he has shunned the modern temptation to present us with a psychological analysis of "mad Shelley," half saint, half crank. He has written the definitive biography of the poet. He has told the whole story (including, one must add, a wealth of new information), and he has told it *con amore,* yet without undue eulogy or apology. There are, of course, sandy stretches of dullness in the book, but these only attest the biographer's thoroughness. In any life of Shelley there are bound to be long and wearisome passages—debts and ever more debts, flight from creditors, ailing children (including Elena Adelaide the insoluble), the persistent nagging of that old bloodsucker William Godwin (philosopher), the dreadful death of Harriet (who drowned herself), and the heartbreaking story of Fanny Imlay (who poisoned herself), and the incredible career of Claire Clairmont, who, after some effort, got herself ruined by Lord Byron and had an ailing child of her own, and Teresa Viviani, an emotional young lady of Pisa who wrote verse and an essay on love, and furnished the inspiration for "Epipsychidion," and Mrs. Jane Williams (who

wasn't really married to Mr. Williams), who played well on
the guitar and equally well with fire, but remained unsinged.
And all the while the dismal undersong furnished by Mary
Shelley (inevitably disillusioned), the Satanic inconsistencies
of Lord Byron, the mingled savagery and sentimentalities of
Trelawny and a dozen other mad folk that hovered round the
angelic rebel!

The reader has throughout it all the feeling of a person who
has blundered into crisis after crisis and brawl after brawl, and
has never found time to settle down and look about him. Shelley
and his family are perpetually—and wisely—on the move, with
plans forever in flux and extending but a month or so into
the future.

But the miracle that is Shelley remains, and it is the miracle
of his lyric poetry. It is the sole thing of abiding importance
about him. Over and above all the coil and confusion of his
slovenly domesticity rises the radiant column of his song. He
is, as Swinburne called him long ago, "the perfect singing god."
He soars away on his luminous pinions till, like the lark, he is
invisible in the sky, though his voice is still heard far overhead:

> The deathless stars are bright above;
> If I would cross the shade of night,
> Within my heart is the lamp of love,
> And that is day!
> And the moon will smile with gentle light
> On my golden plumes where'er they move;
> The meteors will linger round my flight,
> And make night day.

Such are the notes he can "loosen in a silver shower," and he
can do it as often as he feels the impulse, as can the youthful
Mozart.

I am told that certain critics of the new school are "out to get Shelley," and that their aim is similar to that of the horrible debunking school that has had its day. Their aim is similar, but their method is different: they publish prose abstracts and even diagrams of the world-famous lyrics and inquire whether they make sense. They pull the similes in pieces to see if they are good similes. They are the scholars of Laputa. They cast the violet into the crucible, and look for chemical results. It is not so much the philosophy to which they object, for that, repellent as it remains, is more modernistic than it was a hundred years ago. It is apparently the sheer melody which gives offense. I infer, therefore, that they have no ear, or else that they believe that poetry can get along without melody. Little of the commodity is to be found in representatives of the art today; but there is enough and to spare in the old masters, and we may conclude that Shelley will always have his audience, for none, as Beers used to remark, sings so wildly well as the angel Israfel.

Perhaps there is a kind of rift in every poet's character—the singer existing apart from the mere citizen, the suntreader apart from the pedestrian in Piccadilly. It is easy, of course, to work out a connection between the crackbrained young Shelley who bought up the crayfish exposed for sale in the streets of Marlow in order to get them thrown back into the river, and the beautiful and ineffectual author of "Prometheus Unbound" and "The Revolt of Islam." It is amusing to read of how Shelley took off his shoes in order to give them to a wanderer (female) in need; and it is tempting to trace a relation between this eleemosynary act and the doctrines set forth (let us say) in "Rosalind and Helen"; but it is not by such methods that we shall pluck the heart out of the poet's mystery. Indeed, the miracle of Shelley's poetry is hardly encountered in any of the longer poems, except "Adonais," "Epipsychidion," and "The Sensitive Plant." By a simple paradox his long poems may be termed his minor works. It is in the short pieces that the glory of his lyric endowment is fully manifest, and the music that emanates from them appears also in the scraps and fragments of song with which his volumes abound, for there his art is unpremeditated; and according as this lyric impulse dominates the longer poems do they have a value as such.

Professor Ifor Evans, in the latest history of English literature, pronounces "Prometheus Unbound" to be Shelley's greatest work, and the famous skylark ode as "the least characteristic of his poems." Surely such dicta are slightly perverse. "Prometheus Unbound" sets forth no doctrine that is of much importance to radical thinkers today; the whole significance of this astonishing production is that it began as a play and turned into a paean. The music interrupts the action which, at the beginning, is dimly Hellenic, and at last defeats the dramatist altogether, and becomes a prolonged and ecstatic song of triumph. We ignore the "message," as Mr. Evans calls it, but lend a ready ear to the inarticulate music. Indeed, Shelley is never a poet till he abandons ratiocination and surrenders to rapture, or to its counterpart, despair. It is the emotion that gives him

> . . . strength to pierce the guarded wit,
> And pass into the panting heart beneath
> With lightning and with music.

And it is precisely this intangible, this all but indescribable, quality that makes the "Ode to a Skylark" his most characteristic and best-loved poem. It is worth the whole of "Queen Mab" and "The Revolt of Islam" put together.

It is a late day to be praising Shelley's lyrics, which have been hackneyed in every school reader and in every anthology of verse. But the very fact that they get hackneyed is indicative of a great truth about them, and that is that they owe their influence not to any mere interest in the personality of the singer or in the circumstances out of which the poem sprang, but to its appeal to the universal emotion of mankind. Their glory as supreme musical expressions has but little to do with the biographical explanations offered by the commentators, which are very like the program notes provided for an audience that cannot listen to a symphony unaided. The personal references are so idealized that they seem to be somehow a reflection of our own, devised to release the feelings of the "stuffed bosom," and cause us to forget or quite to ignore the original events or personal utterances that may be detected in them. Of what conceivable interest to anybody is it that "Music when soft voices die" was inspired by A or by B, by man or woman, by soprano or by basso profundo? Let any reader make what use of it he may. The "Lines to an Indian Air," once attributed to Byron, better known as "I arise from dreams of thee," have been for decades a lover's song, and sung with delight by generations of college boys who discovered the words with amazement in their textbook.

There is an amusing anecdote of the poet's sojourn at the Baths of San Giuliano (near Pisa), where his residence overlooked the market square. A Mrs. Mason, a friend of the Shelleys, paid them a visit at the time when the poet was at work upon his great "Ode to Liberty," inspired partly by contemporary political events and partly by his glowing dreams of the

future of mankind. This poem Shelley attempted to read aloud
to his visitor. But, as the devil would have it, a sale of pigs was
in uproarious progress in the market below, and noise was as of
Tophet. It was not only the screaming of the Italians but the
screaming of the pigs that rent the air. Now, when a man is
considering the purchase of a particular pig, it is customary,
I am told, to seize the creature smartly by the ear and by the
tail, and test his weight while holding him suspended in air.
Thereupon the resentful animal fills the air with immoderate
squeals of indignation, while the customer wrangles with the
owner regarding the price. Such was the babel below the poet's
windows. Within the house he read aloud the perfervid verses
of his ode. Higher and higher rose the shrill music:

> . . . My soul spurned the chains of its dismay,
>   And in the rapid plumes of song
>   Clothed itself, sublime and strong;
> As a young eagle soars the morning clouds among,
>   Hovering in verse o'er its accustomed prey . . .

Higher and ever higher rose the uproar below.

Momentarily the poet was defeated by the pigs. But the irony
of it did not escape him, for he laughingly compared the obbli-
gato to the chorus of the frogs in Aristophanes. And we, glanc-
ing at the incident over a century after, may detect in it an
irony subtler yet. "Le poète qui chante, et les cochons qui
crient." The Muse against the market place! Harmony struggling with discord—the abiding plight of the poet.

VI

The Poetry of the Brontës

IT is now some years since the Brontës passed their centenary. Charlotte, the eldest of the sisters who came to maturity, was born in 1816, and Anne, the youngest, in 1820; so that they are now well along in the second century of their existence. It is remarkable that there has been no loss of momentum such as is apt to occur after the false excitement caused by the completion of the first hundred years. The three Brontës, like our own Emily Dickinson, are fascinating still. They retain their power of winning devotees. None of them, indeed, has lacked a critic to proclaim her the peculiar genius of the family. Charlotte, from the beginning, has had a host of eager interpreters: Mrs. Gaskell in an earlier generation and Miss Sinclair in a later, have revealed the devotion of one sex; Swinburne (who intimated that she would outlast Dickens) and Mr. A. C. Benson the esteem of the other. Few novelists of the nineteenth century, that great classic era of fiction, have been so laden with praise. As for Emily Brontë, she has had so many admirers that it has become commonplace to "discover" her. *Wuthering Heights* is now one of the most widely read of all novels. Nor has Anne been passed over in the distribution of critical favors. Mr. George Moore once published an essay in the form of a dialogue with Sir Edmund Gosse in which he contended that Anne was the greatest of the three sisters. Thereafter there was no one left to confer genius upon except the demoniac brother, Branwell, and accordingly in 1923 Miss Alice

Law published her theory that Branwell was the real author of *Wuthering Heights,* the abused, cheated, and neglected genius of the Haworth vicarage. This caused a fine flutter in the Brontesque circle (never too peaceful), and threatens English criticism with a Brontë heresy of Baconian quality if not of Baconian proportions. Who knows but we may presently hear of ciphers and acrostic signatures?

Well, it is all very strange, this devotion to the recluses of Yorkshire, the drab, shy girls with the flaming hearts and the teeming imaginations. The theme is romantic enough—the governess racked with heroic passion, a sort of female counterpart of Ruy Blas, the lackey who loved a queen. Some writers seem to feel that romanticism is dead; but the Brontës, who are as romantic as Byron, seem to give the lie to such a view. The Brontës are not dead or even ailing. They are perhaps more alive than their books; at any rate, the result of all this activity of their disciples has been to keep Charlotte and Emily and Anne to the fore, as Frances Henri and Catherine Earnshaw and Agnes Grey recede a little into the background. We know Haworth better than Villette.

But the day will come at last when the old, unhappy tale of the Brontës must be forgotten, and the literary work of the three sisters judged on its merits and not merely prized for the light it throws on their biography. Time knows no chivalries. Literary achievements, not romantic biography, must in the long run be the basis of an enduring place in literary history. Their novels, which are likely to be read long after it has been forgotten that they were all quarried out of their biography, must in the long run be their chief claim to remembrance, stories as powerful as they are strange and crude, yet revealing the splendid paradox of humanity, that out of weakness we may be made strong. And among the readers of these stories there will ever be some who turn their eyes from the prose to the verse, to see if in the lyrics there may perchance exist an expression of their genius free from the extravagance and rawness that mark their fictions.

It is never to be forgotten that their first appearance was as poetesses—or rather as poets—Currer, Ellis, and Acton Bell. The grey-green little volume of *Poems* (1846) was shifted from one publisher to another (to the delight of book collectors) and was unregarded by the public. But there is nothing surprising in the failure of the book, for it is always difficult to detect the half dozen pieces of permanent value among scores of poems issuing out of the unknown. In this case, the confusion was worse because of the triple authorship and the assumption of masculine names by authors obviously female. But though the volume lacked readers in 1846, it has won them since. Mr. A. C. Benson edited the poems judiciously in 1915, and Mr. Clement K. Shorter (who long since appropriated all the Brontës to himself) again in 1925. Whether it is wholly wise to reprint every scrap of verse that escaped the wastepaper basket will seem to the Brontesque admirers an insolent query, but it is a doubt sure to arise in the minds of the critical and the irreverent. The menace to the poetical reputation of the sisters has always been that of suffocation by the second-rate. A few of the poems are of very high quality indeed; some, though marred by blemishes and discords, have a certain value; but others —many others—might be permanently spared, and among these we must fearlessly include the bulk of the new material that Mr. Shorter printed.

The lack which is common to the work of all three is of course that of discipline. These young ladies are disinclined to

wait, to reconsider, to prune, to reject. There is surely some
hereditary relation between the vice of Branwell's life and the
stylistic vices of his sisters. In the poems, as in the novels, emotion is everywhere astir, but always plunging into language,
wreaking itself upon expression, set down hurriedly in all its
rawness, never, by any chance, recollected in tranquillity.
When the Brontës experience an emotion, they out with it.
They consume no smoke. Now to admit all this is, to be sure,
but to assert that they are young. It is in their fervid youth-
fulness that half their charm consists; and yet, after reading
them for a time, one cannot help longing for the professional
touch. One turns perhaps to Landor or to Bridges, to restraint
and reticence, and an experienced artist's sure control of his
instrument. The atmosphere may be chillier but it is also clearer.
The nocturnes and études of the Brontës are always stormy and
moving, but the performer now and again strikes a false note,
and sets the author's nerves quivering. Emily, for example, can
write about the stars in a simple and affecting way,

> I turned me to the pillow then,
>   To call back night and see
> Your worlds of solemn light again
>   Throb with my heart and me.

She could write as well as that, and then she could add:

> The curtains waved, the wakened flies
>   Were murmuring round my room,
> Imprisoned there till I should rise,
>   And give them leave to roam.

A yet more slovenly manner, and a sort of shriekiness that
Emily never betrays, is found in the poems of Currer Bell.

Charlotte's poem, "He saw my heart's woe," might come straight from the most inflamed pages of *Jane Eyre:*

> Idolator I kneeled to an idol cut in rock,
>> I might have slashed my flesh and drawn my heart's best blood,
> The Granite God had felt no tenderness, no shock,
>> My Baal had not seen nor heard nor understood.

This is like the hysteria which flows from the pen of Jane Eyre; you may find it in your heart to wish it all keyed down, but you cannot deny its passion—and then, suddenly all sinks into prose and bathos:

> Now, Heaven, heal the wound which I still deeply feel,
>> Thy glorious hosts look not in scorn on our poor race,
> Thy King eternal doth no iron judgment deal
>> On suffering worms who seek forgiveness, comfort, grace.

The sincerity of this is beyond doubt, but so is the sincerity of the inarticulate cry of pain or pleasure; yet we do not call it artistic. A whole step in the creative process is lacking—the reconsideration by the artist of his first intensities, a willingness to temper and restrain in the interests of technique and an adopted mode of expression.

Of all the group the one who came nearest to self-restraint was Anne. She, the least rebellious, craves direction and control, and finds it in her Christian faith, submitting herself to a higher power. Her verse is prevailingly religious, her mood less violent, her notes few and simple, reminiscent of eighteenth-century hymnals and, in particular, of the poetry of William Cowper. Her verses to the memory of that poet are something more than a girl's sweet tribute to a favorite: they are instinct with the very spirit which she admired in her master, and it is pleasant to feel that, among all the poems

written in his honor, none would have gratified the recluse of
Olney more than these simple lines. Certain of Anne's poems,
such, for example, as "A Prayer."—

> I cannot say my faith is strong,
> I dare not hope my love is great,
> But strength and love to Thee belong,
> Oh, do not leave me desolate,

are sung as hymns by persons who never heard her name. Such
dubious fame would not satisfy Mr. George Moore, but it
would have comforted Anne with the thought that she had not
sung in vain.

But it is hard to give adequate attention to Anne's verse, or
even to Charlotte's tempestuous song when we think of Emily.
It will be found, in the end, if it be not already clear, that the
poetic genius of the family (whatever be Emily's ultimate rank
as a novelist) is concentrated in her. Some half dozen of her
poems—"Remembrance," "The linnet in the rocky dells,"
"Stanzas to ——," "The Old Stoic," "Love and Friendship,"
"The Bluebell," and of course "No coward soul is mine"—are
destined to grow in fame until they establish her poetic reputation upon an enduring albeit narrow base. For Emily had the
gift of song, and had it as indubitably as had Christina Rossetti.
There are passages, indeed, when she is very near in mood and
expression to Miss Rossetti:

> Do I despise the timid deer,
> Because his limbs are fleet with fear?
> Or would I mock the wolf's death-howl,
> Because his form is gaunt and foul?
> Or hear with joy the leveret's cry,
> Because it cannot bravely die?

> No! Then above his memory
> Let Pity's heart as tender be;
> Say, "Earth lie lightly on that breast,
> And, kind Heaven, grant that spirit rest!"

We find at times an unchastened emotionalism in her as we do almost continuously in her elder sister, and there are moments in her verse, as in Charlotte's, when the spirit of Byron seems to be moving her,

> The spirit which bent 'neath its power,
> How it longed—how it burned to be free!
> If I could have wept in that hour,
> Those tears had been heaven to me.

There is an emphasis on "freedom" which one does not always understand; but also a clear resolution to follow the impetus of her own genius, which can be very readily understood and no less readily commended.

> I'll walk where my own nature would be leading:
> It vexes me to choose another guide;
> Where the grey flocks in ferny glens are feeding;
> Where the wild wind blows on the mountain-side.

It is this intense self-confidence that burns through the splendid credo with which she closed her literary if not her earthly life:

> No coward soul is mine,
> No trembler in the world's storm-troubled sphere;
> I see Heaven's glories shine,
> And Faith shines equal, arming me from Fear.

No anthology is now without this poem. Its passionate affirmations are as startling as the passionate denials of Mr. Henley's *Invictus*.

Moreover this "last" poem, as it is convenient to call it, is in other respects characteristic. It issues from the splendid heart of her as she confronts life, wide-eyed, confident, unbroken, though having come out of—nay yet enduring—great tribulation. All her verse is the expression of this, nothing more; for she creates no world beyond or apart from herself. Those childish imaginings which have to do with the mythical "Gondals" inhabiting the distant kingdom of Andora, will deceive nobody. Emily is Emily still, even when she signs herself A. G. Alaisda, even like the youngsters of our own family, who consent to entertain the grown-ups with private theatricals. All the fun is in seeing familiar faces in masquerade, but we do not deceive ourselves into thinking that a histrionic race is arising in our midst. The power of passing out of herself and creating a world of which she had no experience is hers, if at all, only in *Wuthering Heights,* but not in poetry. Charlotte has it. "Gilbert," for example, which is a dreadful, perhaps a contemptible poem, gives some evidence of Charlotte's power as a "maker," and represents a kind of thing entirely lacking in Emily's work. "Gilbert" is essentially a novelist's poem. The conclusion of it might have been written by the youthful Walter Scott for *Tales of Terror;* but, failure as it is, it discloses a power to pass outside herself and transcend her own experience, which differentiates Charlotte's skill from Emily's.

But neither Charlotte nor Anne ever really sings. That gift, the gift of raising her voice in clear, keen melody, is Emily's alone. Her voice, to be sure, has never been "trained," but it is none the less a singing voice.

> The linnet in the rocky dells,
> The moor-lark in the air,

> The bee among the heather bells
> That hide my lady fair,
>
> The wild deer browse above her breast;
> The wild birds raise their brood,
> And they her smiles of love caressed,
> Have left her solitude.

It is in such utterances that one may find a retort to those who, like the present writer in the earlier sections of this paper, are inclined to cavil at the Brontës for their lack of self-discipline and their uncertain technique. The primitive note, the speed and simplicity of the natural voice, is almost never found without plenteous imperfections; but it has beauties of its own. The lyrics of Emily Brontë are childlike, and childlike in a fuller sense than may at first be apparent. They are like children who are always disappointing us, failing to live up to what is expected of them, falling into absurd error that might have been quite simply avoided, and yet all the while possessed of a rare beauty which is transitory and never to be recaptured. It is the strange, the unexpected, that haunts us as we read. It is a quality not to be imitated, hardly to be defined. Who taught her to write such lines as

> Mourn not him whose doom
> Heaven itself is mourning?

Who taught the girl who had known but little joy to write of the mood

> When joy grew mad with awe, at counting future tears?

It is easy to understand that she, who had listened to the wind on the Yorkshire moors, could write of it as uttering

> Wild words of an ancient song,
> Undefined, without a name.

But who taught her, who had passed her narrow life in the midst of death, whose years were few and stricken with grief, to write in the end,

> There is not room for Death,
> Nor atom that his might could render void?

The secret is locked fast in the girl's heart; and it is the hope of spelling it that will draw readers to her for many years to come.

VII

William Morris as Poet

An Address delivered before the Yale Library Associates. 1934.

IN the year 1858, a modest volume entitled *The Defence of Guenevere, and Other Poems* was printed at the Chiswick Press for Bell and Daldy, publishers. Despite its drab binding, it was a prettily printed volume, displaying a liberal use of ornamental capitals and head and tail pieces, appropriate enough to the verses of a young artist in his early twenties, which were still for him formative years. He had recently completed his picture, painted in the pre-Raphaelite manner, entitled "Queen Guenevere." Both painting and poem were the result of the same impulse, a passionate conviction that the life of the Middle Ages was the most fertile inspiration of the fine arts. The little volume was dedicated to "Dante Gabriel Rossetti, Painter," and displayed throughout the devotion of an ardent disciple. Readers of it soon discovered that four of the poems were the counterpart of four water-color drawings by Rossetti. Two of them, "The Blue Closet" and "The Tune of Seven Towers" will remain significant as experiments in the difficult attempt to translate one art into another. The poems are perhaps as near to painting as it is possible for verse to come. They have the same violent color contrasts as the pictures from which they derive, and are involved in the same atmosphere of passion, intense but exotic and wistful. Everything seems to be death-stricken at the root. Tall damozels, with enormous eyes and luscious lips (never visited by a smile), play upon strange instruments of music, viols, citoles, and lutes, and the ladies seem to be enclosed within some magic chamber far from the world we know.

> Alice the Queen and Louise the Queen,
> Two damozels wearing purple and green,
> Four lone ladies dwelling here
> From day to day and year to year.

Like the figures in a picture by Burne-Jones, they all seem to be under the influence of a spell, and the songs that they sing are not of this world, though just beyond their retreat (or their prison) is the howling tumult of the tumbling seas.

If it were necessary to find a link between the paintings of Rossetti and those of Burne-Jones, it might be found in these very poems of Morris. In 1858, the original pre-Raphaelite brotherhood had practically ceased to exist; but now in the poems of Morris and the paintings of Burne-Jones their influence suddenly sprang into new and vigorous life.

As there were poems in the book inspired by painting, so there were poems that might themselves be easily translated into pre-Raphaelite pictures. In "The Sailing of the Sword," for example, three ladies watch the departure of their three knights, as the good ship, the *Sword,* puts out to sea.

> Alicia wore a scarlet gown,
>   *When the Sword went out to sea,*
> But Ursula's was russet brown:
>   For the mist we could not see
> The scarlet roofs of the good town,
>   *When the Sword went out to sea.*

Green holly in Alicia's hand,
  When the Sword went out to sea;
With sere oak-leaves did Ursula stand;
  O! yet alas for me!
I did but bear a peel'd white wand,
  When the Sword went out to sea.

O, russet brown and scarlet bright,
  When the Sword went out to sea,
My sisters wore; I wore but white:
  Red, brown, and white are three;
Three damozels; each had a knight,
  When the Sword went out to sea.

But it is not merely to an exotic garden of love that the young
poet invites us: he never forgets, to be sure, that love of woman
is the best thing that life has to offer a man. The title which
he gave to a later volume, *Love Is Enough,* might be applied to
much of what he wrote, save the handful of poems which he
composed for the Socialist party many years later. Love is
enough, but it is not all. There is the wine of battle with a
hated foe for man to drink. He must know the fierce delight of
breaking up an enemy's plate armor or slaughtering him with
his hands. To this very thing, indeed, the love of ladies inspires him:

My hand was steady, too, to take
My axe from round my neck, and break
John's steel coat up for my love's sake.

Morris delighted in such phases of the Middle Ages as the
rather pallid romanticism of Tennyson had deliberately thrust
to one side. The boy was interested in the crashing activity of
medieval life, its tournaments and jousts, its blazing towns and

angry mobs, not in the opportunities that it afforded for illustrating high ethical truths. Morris' "Defence of Guenevere" is so much more advanced a poem than Tennyson's idyl on the same subject that it is hard to realize that it actually preceded the publication of the laureate's story, but so it is. Tennyson's lofty tone and his concern for the sanctities of the Victorian home—in an idyl which might more properly be entitled "The Defence of Arthur," than "Guinevere"—are far more antiquated today than the young passion and the subtle eloquence of Morris' splendid "Guenevere." Tennyson had not yet printed any of *The Idylls of the King,* except the "Morte d'Arthur," but his pretty medievalism was already familiar, and its intense popularity invited a protest from such as knew that period better. The protest was perhaps hastened by the publication of a book which brought renewed fame to the pleasant dreams of the long ago and the far away that characterize the early work of the laureate. This book was a new edition of Tennyson's poems, published by Edward Moxon in 1857, which was sumptuously illustrated by the chief artists of England. Prominent among them were the three original pre-Raphaelites, Rossetti, Holman Hunt, and Millais, who furnished thirty out of the fifty-three illustrations. Rossetti drew the designs for the poems supposed to be especially medieval, "The Lady of Shalott," "Mariana in the South," "The Palace of Art," and "Sir Galahad."

These drawings are exquisitely pre-Raphaelite, and in every case much more amorous and intense than the poems which they accompany and interpret. One wonders what Tennyson thought of the first illustration for "The Palace of Art," which represents a damozel with flowing hair, her long hands resting on the keys of a medieval organ, as her head is drawn backward

by her lover, who has surprised her at her music, and now im-
prints passionate kisses above her eyes which are closed in
ecstasy. The drawing of Sir Galahad at the shrine of the Holy
Grail is as beautiful a thing as Rossetti ever made; but the
youth is much more knight than acolyte. With these wood-
cuts Morris was of course intimately acquainted, and by them
he was profoundly influenced. The poems of Tennyson for
which they were made must have seemed much more feeble and
watery than the pictures, and a travesty of medievalism. Tennyson's Galahad, for example, utters the following sentiments:

> I never felt the kiss of love,
>   Nor maiden's hand in mine,
> More bounteous aspects on me beam,
>   Me mightier transports move and thrill,
> So keep I fair thro' faith and prayer
>   A virgin heart in work and will.

What manner of young prig is this? A thing of wax, the
ideal boy of clerical schoolmasters, but certainly no medieval
knight. Over against such a lay figure Morris set his own Sir
Galahad, who rather resents having to be a virgin knight:

> If Father Lancelot ride out,
>   Can he not think of Guenevere's arms, round
> Warm and lithe, about his neck, and shout
>   Till all the place grows joyful with the sound?

> And when he lists, can often see her face,
>   And think, "Next month I kiss you, or next week,
> And still you think of me," therefore the place
>   Grows very pleasant, whatsoever he seek.

There is a refreshing savageness in certain poems which reveals the young poet's earnest desire to discover what battle

was actually like in the fifteenth century. He describes, for instance, a boy of fifteen as fighting in the streets of Beauvais,
where his father, chuckling even as he slaughters, bids him
count the number of women's corpses lying about; but it is too
much for the boy who is already faint with smelling the burnt
bones from a great fire in Beauvais Church. Morris wished it
known that he was aware that there might be a bright intoxica-
tion in the killing of men, as there is a delight in the hunting
of wild beasts. Thus the father in "Shameful Death" avenges
the murder of his son:

> But I met Sir John of the Fen
>   Long ago on a summer day,
> And am glad to think of the moment when
>   I took his life away.

The most powerful of these poems, and one destined to last
as long as any of them is "The Haystack in the Floods," a story
of murder in cold blood, melodramatic in the extreme, but
with a vividness of detail which a more famous realist might
have been proud to own. The story is reduced to its lowest
terms. The scene which the poet paints is evidently the bare
climax of a situation which, if explained at length, would
approach the proportions of a novel.

A knight, Sir Robert, and his lady, Jehane, of whose past we
know nothing, fall into an ambush laid for them by their
mortal enemy, Godmar, who is the lady's rejected lover. If she
now refuses to renounce Sir Robert, Godmar will send her
back to Paris where she will be tried as a witch (why we are
not told), and then submitted to trial by ordeal, thrown into the
water to sink or swim, or perhaps burned at the stake. After a
long sleep in the dank hayfield, she at last awakes and gives

her refusal point blank. Thereupon Godmar proceeds to his
vengeance,

> With a start
> Up Godmar rose, thrust them apart;
> From Robert's throat he loosed the bands
> Of silk and mail; with empty hands
> Held out, she stood and gazed, and saw
> The long bright blade without a flaw
> Glide out from Godmar's sheath, his hand
> In Robert's hair; she saw him bend
> Back Robert's head; she saw him send
> The thin steel down; the blow told well,
> Right backward the knight Robert fell,
> And moaned as dogs do, being half dead,
> Unwitting, as I deem; so then
> Godmar turned grinning to his men,
> Who ran, some five or six, and beat
> His head to pieces at their feet.

This is melodrama, no doubt, but it is neatly and even power-
fully fashioned. I cannot understand how any reviewer of the
volume could have failed to appreciate its originality and its
promise. "Originality" I say, for it is surprisingly independent
—amazingly so for a book archaic in kind. An investigation of
its "sources" hardly repays the effort that must be expended
upon it. "Promise" I say, because any intelligent reader must
have felt that here was the debut of a narrative poet of distinction, devoted to a study of the life of the Middle Ages, with a
delight in their beauty that equaled Tennyson's and a conception of their brutal passions that equaled Browning's. I do not
know that any reviewer of the time set up a comparison with
Chaucer; but it would not have been wholly inept, and cer-

tainly nothing would have been more pleasing to the poet. For it was not Scott, or even Malory to whom Morris gave his allegiance, but rather Chaucer. He proclaimed Chaucer his master, and for his next literary venture he designed a framework like that of *The Canterbury Tales*.

In *The Earthly Paradise* there were to be twenty-four tales of varying length, and a long prologue giving an account of the persons supposed to be telling the stories. Greek and Germanic tales alternately, diversified with lyrics, and held together by bits of narrative—such was Morris' plan. It was not so extensive as Chaucer's or Boccaccio's, but nobody would call it modest. Unlike Chaucer's, the plan was destined to be fully realized, and realized within a decade. The first twelve tales were published in 1868, just ten years after *The Defence of Guenevere* and the last twelve in 1870. It is a production of forty thousand lines in all—a bulk larger than that of the *Iliad* and the *Odyssey* combined. It would be difficult to cite a record of poetic achievement more nimble than this.

But even these statistics do scant justice to the man's amazing productivity. One of the Greek tales for the first part of *The Earthly Paradise* was to have been the story of Jason and the Golden Fleece. Morris had no difficulty in producing it. He never had any difficulty in producing anything. He knew neither lethargy nor hesitation, but found that the more he wrote, the more he had to write. That artistic economy of means which he had learned from Rossetti's ballads, and which had been so conspicuous a grace in *The Defence of Guenevere,* departed from him at once and forever. The story of Jason became so long that it could not be included in *The Earthly Paradise* at all but had to be put forth as a separate volume, *The Life and Death of Jason, a Poem in Seventeen Books.*

At this time his brain teemed with plans of epic magnitude. He published, as has been said, half *The Earthly Paradise* during 1868, in a stout black volume containing 676 pages of verse. The titles intended for the second half were announced on a page of advertisement at the end, than which nothing could be more indicative of our poet's nature. Half the tales there listed he never wrote, not because he could not, but because other and ever larger plans got in his way. And so the story of "Theseus" went by the board, and "Orpheus and Eurydice," and "Dorothea" (presumably the story of the martyrdom of that popular saint), and "The Dolphins and the Lovers," and "Amys and Amillion." Speed sat upon his flying quill. In two years the second half of *The Earthly Paradise* was ready, but lo, a single volume was no longer adequate. There were now nearly a thousand pages, filling two more squat black volumes. The longest of the tales, "The Lovers of Gudrun," as well as several others, had formed no part of the original plan, but were added for good measure, as the poet went along. There are over five thousand lines in "The Lovers of Gudrun," which is thus half as long again as the *Beowulf*.

In view of this inveterate fertility, the poet's description of himself in the prefatory verses began to seem ironic enough, and Morris was accounted his harshest if not his most preposterous critic. How any poet whose work already dwarfed Homer's could speak of himself as an idle singer passed all conception. How could any man who must have given days and nights to copying out his verses possibly speak of his days as idle? His poems he described as "not too importunate," and this is exact enough. His tales do not beset our attention, but rise before it like some warm mirage. They seem to come from some lotos-land, in which it is always afternoon. As the poet himself asserts, they are sung

> To those who in the sleepy region stay,
> Lulled by the singer of an empty day.

Here surely is irony and to spare. That the most vigorous and productive man of his time should write poems which instill an invincible languor in our spirits is one of the paradoxes of the literature. Whence this narcotic melancholy that reigns over his pages?

> Weep, O Love, the days that flit,
>   Now while I can feel thy breath,
> Then may I remember it
>   Sad and old and near my death,
> Kiss me, love! for who knoweth
>   What thing cometh after death?

It would be futile to deny that this is the keynote of *The Earthly Paradise,* and it is for this reason that the poet's desire to be remembered as a follower of Chaucer is fraught with such peril. For where, one will ask, is the abounding vigor of Chaucer, his normality, his faith in the essential goodness and significance of life? Where is Chaucer's humor? Where is there so much as a hint of that panoramic *comédie humaine* which is the lustrous glory of *The Canterbury Tales?* He would be a rash critic who should assert that Morris added a single character to English literature. How extraordinary that he who delighted in the companionship of men should have lacked this power of creation! How strange that he who played so prominent and noble a role in the life of his age should have drawn from it no single story of the contemporary world of which he knew so much. His face is turned from his own world, and he was content to remain as a teller of twice-told tales.

A recurrent theme in *The Earthly Paradise* is that of the hero who, through some lucky accident of Fate, becomes involved in a quest for a divine maiden or goddess throned in an inaccessible and perilous tract of fairyland. She is ringed round with fiery dangers, like Brunhilde or the Sleeping Beauty, awaiting the kiss of an all-conquering knight to waken her into life. She is often a *belle dame sans merci,* who receives her thrall into a paradise of love and inaction, where he experiences for a time such joys as the soul of man knoweth not, but which withdraw him forever from the sweet commonplace of human existence. This, in one form or another, is the theme of half the stories in the collection. You find it in "Ogier the Dane," in "The Hill of Venus" (familiar to us all as the Tannhäuser myth); you have it in "The Land East of the Sun and West of the Moon," in "The Watching of the Falcon," in "The Lady of the Land," in "The Man Born to Be King," in "Atalanta's Race," and in "Pygmalion and the Image." However vivid and truthful such situations may have been to the original myth-makers from whom the stories come, they fade, under the hand of Morris, into figures in a tapestry or (where he himself placed them) in a lovely dream, but a dream without power upon the reader. Unlike John Keats, who was possessed by the same dream of love perfect and unattainable, Morris was incapable of using the ancient myths to reveal the abiding issues of love and death, so that they shall renew their life in our modern world, and hold again high place in the human heart. But such power is given only to the highest.

The second half of *The Earthly Paradise* made it clear that Morris' interest was passing from the medieval to the Icelandic world. In the interval between the two parts, he had translated into prose two of the most important of the great Norse sagas, *The Story of Grettir,* and *The Story of the Volsungs and Niblungs.* Yet a third, the splendid *Laxdale Saga,* is the source of the tale of "The Lovers of Gudrun," already mentioned. From this time forth William Morris was to be the great advocate of Norse studies in England. Of his activity and his success I shall not speak; but of his long poem, *Sigurd the Volsung,* something must be said, because it represents the final stage in his poetic development. It is a version of the great Icelandic legend in archaic language and in hexameter verse of alternating iambic and anapaestic character. It is in four great parts, and traces the plot through the exploits of Sigmund down to the final vengeance of Gudrun.

Sigurd the Volsung is as Norse as the poet could make it. He traveled twice to Iceland while he was at work upon it, in search of local color, and loved the story with an intensity which no reader of the original Norse saga can fail to understand. But the poem, published in 1876, met, as Professor Beers intimated, with no general acceptance; it proved to be much less popular than *The Earthly Paradise.* For in spite of Morris' fidelity to his sources and in spite of that bracing wind from the north which, according to Mr. Holbrook Jackson, blows over these pages, they remain remote and unrealized. It is, to be sure, a better story than the farrago which Wagner used for his trilogy, but for those who love the tale, the Norse version is "the thing itself," and the modern reworkings of it but pastiche.

In his apparent conviction that the body of Germanic legend was a sufficient basis for modern English poetry, Morris chose not to reckon with that vast tributary stream which flowed north and westward from the shores of the Mediterranean, bringing with it the transforming influence of the Christian Church, and, in almost equal majesty and power, the culture of Greece and Rome. In the light of these, England had walked since the days of Patrick and Augustine; and in the light of these Morris had begun his work as a poet. But the first of them he renounced in early manhood, and the second in middle age. Therefore his career as a poet reveals a progressive impoverishment, a retreat from the modern world and the ordinary interests of men, until he is left at last a stark and isolated figure upon a rocky island amid the mists of the northern seas.

VIII

The Amusing
Pre-Raphaelites

SOME years ago, in the full flush of a pre-Raphaelite enthusiasm, I journeyed out to Hammersmith and presented myself at the door of Kelmscott House. Morris, I knew, had been dead for years, but it was my hope that enough of the furnishing of the house remained to give me a correct notion of the glories with which he had once surrounded himself. I crossed the threshold with expectant reverence. My courteous host assured me that I had come to the wrong place; that the house which Morris built and furnished as the proper setting for his beautiful wife was far from Hammersmith and its commonplaceness, and that this was merely a London residence and workshop. But that was exactly what I wished to see; for it was the belief of the faithful in those days that the desert of Hammersmith was to blossom like the pre-Raphaelite rose. I passed from room to room with growing uneasiness. It was clear that this house, however great had been the alterations which had befallen it since the death of Morris, had never blossomed at all. Here and there, to be sure, were lovely bits—I remember the orange arbor wallpaper in the dining room and a length or two of the famous fabric, called the "strawberry thief," I think, that served as a bed curtain—but it was slowly borne in upon me that I was not to see the house of my dreams, or, for that matter, of Morris' dreams either. It was obviously just a house to live in, a house where there were the usual inconveniences to be put up with. The pre-Raphaelites, I saw, had had mops and coal scuttles, like the rest of us, and it occurred to me that their names were—literally—Brown and Jones, and, at best, Hunt and Morris. There was Rossetti, of course, as a comforting exception. He had been named for a poet and an archangel. Dante Gabriel was a name romantic enough for any artist—indeed, it seemed a bit too much so when one glanced at Watts' portrait of him, which was disconcertingly stolid, with nothing whatever of Dante's fire or the Angel Gabriel's glory.

Oh, I grant you that I had discovered nothing more important than that the pre-Raphaelites were human; but, you see, I had expected something so very different. I do not say that if I had been permitted to call upon Miss Christina Rossetti I should have expected to find her seated upon a dais of silk and down, "hung with vair and purple dyes," like a princess in one of her brother's pictures; but somewhere, oh! decidedly somewhere, in that room I should have expected to come suddenly upon some bit of ivory, carved with pomegranates and silver grapes and peacocks with a hundred eyes. So much at least. As for the lady herself, it was not too much to hope that she might be a wistful St. Dorothea, like one of Burne-Jones' tall, stiff ladies in painted glass. But Miss Rossetti's house in Torrington Square, which I visited afterward, certainly had no dais and no pictured peacocks, though I seem to remember a grate which was inclined to be smoky. In such a spot in Bloomsbury—or in such spots there and elsewhere— had Miss Rossetti written her lovely hymns and sonnets. In a word, I learned that the pre-Raphaelites had fetched up their pearls of price out of the London sea of ugliness all about them. They did not, it was clear, live in a world of their own glorified upholstery. Like the rest of us, they existed in the midst of sordid embarrassments, unpaid bills, colds in the head, refractory parlor maids, and chimneys that wouldn't draw. For me it was no inconsiderable discovery, this realization of the daily contact of my gods with the horror of Gower Street and the inanities of Chelsea. Why, they could have lived and worked at the corner of Seventh Avenue and Twenty-third Street.

And as I had found my pre-Raphaelites, in some sense, dwelling in a commonplace world, so I was destined to discover in their work an unconsciously comic note. I had, I think, known from the beginning that there was something odd about them, yet I would hardly admit it even to myself. But gradually I came to feel that the ladies were undeniably queer; their eyes were too bulgy and their necks were often too swanlike to be wholly beautiful. Glorious Gabriel had such a passion for full lips that he frequently bestowed upon his ladies mouths so lusciously developed as to be somewhat mawkish. And then there was their hair. Rapunzel, who had hair that streamed all the way to the foot of her tower, was plainly the ideal.

In time one even came to wonder whether life could be so interminably wistful as these pre-Raphaelite people found it. Whatever they did revealed the hidden want, the thoughts too deep for tears, and the divine despair whereof the poets sing. If they laid orange branches on beds, they did it wistfully; if they looked over parapets or sang in blue closets or met their own specters in an enchanted wood, they were wistful still. It was clear that life was not what you chose to make it. Heaven itself, with its blessed damozels, where the queen sits weaving

with her five handmaidens, whose names are five sweet sym-
phonies, is the eternal home of this unfulfilled desire. As the
damozel leans over the gold bar of heaven, warm beneath her
touch, she longs for her earthly lover. He heard her tears. There
are lines in the poem which make you think of Fra Angelico
and Andrea Orcagna. The lover is promised the sight of

> clear-ranged unnumbered heads,
>   Bowed with their aureoles;

and angels, meeting him after his reunion with the beloved, are
to sing

> To their citherns and citoles.

But there is a difference; for the medieval painter conceived
of the ranged order of saints as having safely reached a home,
whereas the Blessed Damozel longs

> Only to live as once on earth
>   With love—only to be,
> As then a while, for ever now
>   Together, I and he.

To descend to less unspeakable things, there was the same
utter strangeness in the poems and paintings that dealt with
earth. Look at the picture in the South Kensington Museum,
called "How They Met Themselves" and try to say how or
why this dread encounter with the *Doppelgänger* has come
about. Or those four ladies in the "Blue Closet." Why, oh, why,
are they there? What has happened? And what is going to
happen?

> Alas! the sea-salt oozes through
> The chinks of the tiles of the Closet Blue;

And ever the great bell overhead
Booms in the wind a knell for the dead,
The wind plays on it a knell for the dead.

Such are the explanations which one pre-Raphaelite brother
gives of the work of another. The poem is Morris'; the picture,
on which the poem was based, is Rossetti's. It now hangs in the
Tate Gallery. You would do well not to press too ardently for
pre-Raphaelite explanations. Why in one picture is the lovely
lady combing her golden hair in the parlor, and why is a youthful queen (in a painting by Val Prinsep) eating bread and
honey in the pre-Raphaelite pantry? Alas! the sea-salt of the
workaday world oozes through the chinks of the tiles of the
Closet Blue! It is as though glimpses of Hammersmith and
Chelsea were to be seen through the broken arches and the
casement windows. When I look at Millais' picture of the death
of Ophelia I can never wholly rid my mind of the story that
Miss Siddal posed for him in a bathtub, and that there was a
cold in the head to pay for it all. I don't mean that I wholly
sympathize with Mr. Max Beerbohm's question, "And what
were they going to do with the Grail when they found it, Mr.
Rossetti?" but I do mean to say that if the pre-Raphaelites shall
be found to have made a permanent contribution to the history of English art and literature, they must go down to posterity with their (not unlovable) follies upon their heads. No
doubt they will go in their glory, too, and with their singing
robes about them; they will be strong enough to bear the burden of their own oddities and their occasional ridiculousness.
But bear it they must. That is the inexorable law of life.

There is at the moment, I suspect, a tendency to belittle the
ecstasies and the wistfulness of the pre-Raphaelites. Their

gilded backgrounds and their wan elongations, their apparent
desire to introduce the emotions of the Song of Solomon into
the daily life of Putney and Hammersmith, their denatured
medievalism—all these things and many more are very far out
of style in our brutal days. But a later generation will estimate
them more fairly. They will not forget to whom we owe it
that color and line and passion were possible in the age of
brick and gas. They could still dream, even while Huxley lectured, and if they sometimes muttered the most excruciatingly
funny things in the midst of their fairest dreams, we will not
forget the glory of it all, even while we are chuckling at the
nonsense.

It is some such mood as that, I fancy, which animates the
great caricaturist who, just as our pre-Raphaelites seemed about
to be forgotten and the prices of their paintings and first edi-
tions were falling in the auction rooms, recalls them to our
minds and our affections with his delicious caricatures entitled
Rossetti and His Circle. I should be very much surprised if
Mr. Beerbohm were not an ardent admirer of our ecstatic
friends. I should, in particular, be much surprised, and even
grieved, if I thought that he did not wholly respect the sad and
saintly figure of Miss Rossetti. There is no slightest reason to
consider him lacking in any such respect. Surely, you will not
think him scornful when he draws a picture of Gabriel and
Christina surrounded by the rainbow glories of fabrics from
some new shop in Regent Street. The brother tries hard to
prevail on his younger sister to accept at any rate one of these
and have a dress made of it from designs to be furnished by
himself:

D. G. R. "What *is* the use, Christina, of having a heart like a singing bird and a water-shoot and all the rest of it, if you insist on getting yourself up like a pew-opener?"

C.R. "Well, Gabriel, I don't know—I'm sure you yourself always dress very quietly."

Or take the picture of Topsy and Ned Jones seated on the settle in the studio where they had worked in Red Lion Square. The caricature reveals at once the significance and the ridiculousness of the pre-Raphaelite movement. The gloriously decorated settle, covered with angels playing on citherns and citoles, contrasts strikingly with the undraped window, the broom in the corner, deal table, and bread loaf, as it does with the figures which are seated upon it, Topsy Morris and Mr. Edward B. Jones, with their incredible hair and whiskers. In the pictures of Rossetti there is a continuous emphasis on the heaviness and stolidity of the elder pre-Raphaelite, as though Mr. Beerbohm wished to insist upon the contrast between this grocerlike figure and the wan loveliness of his pictured ladies. It is surely not un-useful to dwell on such aspects of Rossetti, if they direct our attention to the strangeness of the pre-Raphaelite phenomenon in mid-Victorian England.

Thus Mr. Beerbohm's caricatures become, in a way, a sketch of the movement—one might perhaps venture to call it an interpretation. In him rather than in Mr. Gosse or Mr. William Michael Rossetti (each of whom had a slight connection with the movement), the pre-Raphaelites find a critic who is near enough to them to have a loving intimacy such as only a contemporary can have and yet has also something of the withering sanity of a later generation. Mr. Beerbohm makes us roar with laughter at our old friends and, perhaps, at our old selves; but there is nothing unkindly in the laughter. It is a little like looking at a collection of old photographs which make us feel that the dear queer old creatures whom they represent lived a life which it is well for us not to forget and gave us something that has become a part of ourselves. That something is so truly at one with what is best in us that we can afford to chuckle at the eccentricities of its earliest manifestations. Those people are so well known that they may safely be caricatured. The pre-Raphaelites might conceivably have had a more indulgent critic than Mr. Beerbohm, but surely no juster one. For he has anticipated posterity.

IX

Meredith's Poetry

Written as an introduction to the Altschul Collection of the Works of George Meredith. 1931.

THE appearance of Mr. Altschul's catalogue prompts an inquiry as cynical as it is natural, "Who now reads Meredith?" What is the state of the author's reputation today? It is the challenge of oblivion, addressed, as it were, to an earlier school of enthusiasts. A new generation has arisen that knows not Joseph, and to whom the poet's name is indicative of a way of thought long since a little stale. Can the author make head against the slow obscuring of time, and win readers and disciples in a new age?

It is indeed a question to be asked—a question that is bound to be asked whether we like it or not, for our poet cannot hope for a revocation of the law of nature. His work, like that of his peers of old, must cease to be contemporary and challenging; his disciples, themselves grown a bit aged, must be content to see the shadows settle down upon the work of the master, even as some future time may see him submitted to the ignominy of notes and critical commentary and all the paraphernalia of scholarship. It is a universal law in the literary world. Such are the conditions of survival.

But as Meredith recedes into the past, he may hope, like the others, to be seen in clearer perspective. He will be neither a symbol of the stupid neglect of the masses, nor yet the idol of a literary clique, led by W. M. Rossetti and Sir Edmund Gosse. Readers in future will hardly be concerned over the reputed indifference of the Victorians. Insofar as he is seen against that background, he will stand out in bold relief. He will never be confused with his contemporaries. And it is for his blitheness of spirit that he will be chiefly distinguished among them: for the "volley of ringing laughter" that is heard above his comic scene, for the conversational gaiety of intellectual aristocrats engaged in battle royal of the wits, and for that love of nature which extends downward to its mechanical laws and accepts even its destructiveness with a satisfaction surpassing that of Epictetus.

In him there is neither whining nor evasion. He accepts without dismay or tears of regret. What must he have thought of Tennyson's enfeebled faith and larger hope, of Clough's perpetual reconsideration of a faith that he had already given up for lost, of his friend Thomson's blasphemous despair? He was one of the first to accept all the conclusions of the new scientific and materialistic conception of the universe, but he accepts without surrender of his independence as a thinker. He does not sit in a posture of bereavement, waiting for "Science" to tell him what must be the limits of his sphere of thought. He has his own "reading of earth." And in that reading his emotions and aspirations have their place, but one harmonious with the conception as a whole. He looks, for example, upon death with wide, clear eyes, and accepts it as good, and even desirable. Shall he fear to lay him down in that bosom whence has sprung the rose? Yet he has no sentimentalism at all. He is as invigorating as the April wind. His fondness for a cold breeze sweeping across the downs has been noticed by more than one of his critics as being, in truth, emblematic of the man. He rejoices because the wind is destructive as well as invigorating. For he would not blink the harshness of the theme, the terror of the natural order and the world of blood and tears:

> Weep, bleed, rave, writhe, be distraught,
> She is moveless.

The austere mother, like Demeter who laid a child in the live coals, will teach her offspring to endure hard weather. He is her "great venture," and there are moments when she shall seem to him

> A Mother of aches and jests:
> Soulless, heading a hunt,
> Aimless except for a meal.

And there is a sense in which man, like man's faith in nature, is on trial. Has he the courage and the enduring power of the true disciple, the hard athlete?

> He may entreat, aspire,
> He may despair, and she has never heed,
> She drinking his warm sweat will soothe his need,
> Not his desire.

It is in that very desire, in the restlessness of man's spirit, his dauntless aspiration, that man truly becomes himself and co-operates with the mother who bore him in the fierce struggle that leads toward a perfect union of nature with spirit. "Earth's lustihood pressing to sprout"—that is the significant thing, the exponent of the hidden life of nature, in which

> Flesh unto spirit must grow.

With that consummation will come peace, for "Spirit raves not for a goal," being itself the goal.

It is in this respect that Meredith is likely to encounter his harshest criticism from the radical thinkers of our time; for, disguise the matter as we may, the undeniable fact is that Meredith has a certain faith in progress. He will hold out no romantic hopes to man, whose dream of personal immortality is a nursery fable, useful, no doubt, at one time in his development, but now to be put aside with other childish fancies. But, when all allowances have been made, the fact remains that it is man's highest endowment to descry an "Over-Reason" in the universe, a supernal Mind, toward which man, grown also to be the embodiment of mind, may strive, and so find his reward in "the bliss of his headship of strife." Twist this philosophy how you may, it remains a faith, a faith, to be sure, on trial, but whose issue is no less certain than the renaissance of the earth in spring. Thus it is that Meredith, who on his eightieth birthday wished to be remembered as having delivered himself freely "of very radical sentiments," is, when considered by modern standards, not radical at all.

All this will of course be repudiated by a school of thinkers whose leaders teach that the universe is "headed towards an irrational end, with an utter indifference to human needs and values." Just how Meredith would adjust himself to a science that asserts that nature has produced a phenomenon which has no significance and requires no explanation, we shall never know; nor has any writer of our day his ability to sweep such a conclusion blithely to one side. What would he make of a science that talked of "accidents," and of man as "brought into temporary being by the mere accidental back splash of the torrent of destruction"?

For lassitude, for capitulation, for the tear of sentimentalism Meredith has no place. For such nonsense, excision is the only

cure. Let man rise in native fortitude and confront the force
that he does not understand; let him, if he can find a way,
coöperate with it as a good, but let him not throw himself
prone before it. For the suicide of an Empedocles he has only
contempt—"the last of him was heels in air"—what an ending!

> He leaped. With none to hinder,
> Of Aetna's fiery scoriae
> In the next vomit-shower, made he
>   A more peculiar cinder.
> And this great Doctor, can it be,
> He left no saner recipe
> For men at issue with despair?
> Admiring, even his poet owns,
> While noting his fine lyric tones,
> The last of him was heels in air!

Over the great Doctor's suicide rings out the volley of silvery
laughter.

A generation conceiving of the physical universe as the mani-
festation of a torrent of destruction will think of Meredith as
a conservative, and of his passion for the earth and her destiny
as smacking of a belief almost as absurd as religious faith. Nor
will it be concerned vitally with his *comédie humaine,* for
comedy which deals so largely in accident, nevertheless knows
nothing of a world which must itself be conceived as accidental.
The comic muse, so dear to Meredith, the lady of his worship
and the goddess of his desire, knows accident only because
she knows law, and laughs at blunders only because she is aware
of standards. Hence it is that her laughter is silvery.

One may close the pages of Meredith's comedies with a feeling that in spite of his rather ridiculous airs and graces, in
spite of the conversational gaieties that border upon sheer

euphuism, he has done well by humanity. It is not only mother nature that wins his esteem, but man as well. Diana Warwick, it will be remembered, was a novelist:

"I wonder whether the world is as bad as a certain class of writers tell us!" she sighed in weariness, and mused on their soundings and probings of poor humanity, which the world accepts for the very bottom-truth if their dredge brings up sheer refuse of the abominable. The world imagines those to be at our nature's depths who are impudent enough to expose its muddy shallows.

Meredith's human comedy is gay and aristocratic and clever and self-confident because he deems it a privilege to have been a human being. In this, as in his attitude to nature, he is an optimist. He casts his vote in the affirmative. But that is not all. He believes it worth while to vote. He believes that there is an issue, and takes sides with the easy confidence of a clear-headed, good-natured partisan.

"We that have good wits," mused Touchstone long ago, "have much to answer for." Meredith, too, as one of the wits, has much to answer for. He must answer for constantly distracting the reader from the subject to his mere cleverness of diction and metaphor; he must answer for his habit of leading the reader a merry chase, in which the author always wins, that leaves the reader wondering whether anybody can relish this staccato wit quite as much as its practitioner does. Yet, when all is said, it is a fine compliment which Meredith pays the reader, for he makes the courteous assumption that he has good wits and is willing to use them. Poets, he tells us, "spring imagination with a word or phrase." This is his aim in writing, to invigorate and delight his reader by bringing him into a state where response shall be a genuine activity of mind and admiration a flattering sense of a certain kinship with the author.

With qualities such as these Meredith may bid defiance to the lapsed disciples who conceive of his day as past, and enter into the domain of the classics and the second century of his existence with a serene conviction that he will always hold an audience so long as English readers shall admire good wits in company with good spirits, and a knowledge of the heart in union with an inextinguishable delight in the eternal comedy of human life

The Poetry
of A. E. Housman

IT is unusual for a poet to cultivate his reputation by a policy of silence. It seems strange that one should create an appetite for a particular kind of verse, and then deliberately refuse to gratify it. Nevertheless, in such a policy there may be a kind of weary wisdom, as of one who has apprehended the awful dangers of satiety. In the creation of a public demand for one's work—even for poetry—there is nothing very unusual. Many in this century, whose names still recur, have had their bright day, have formed their little circle, created a demand, satisfied it, and then passed into oblivion. Men in later middle age can well remember when the appetite for Mr. Kipling's poetry seemed insatiable. That demand was fully met, and the poet, whose collected verse now fills a stout volume of nearly a thousand pages, has passed into (perhaps temporary) eclipse. For the moment, nobody, not even his King, will do him any reverence. And those who remember the rise and decline of poor, dear, dead Stephen Phillips have a poignant theme on which to meditate: for what seemed fresher and more fragrant in its day than "Marpessa"? But Mr. Phillips, alas, wrote himself out, and died, I make no doubt, of a broken heart. A dozen cases, nearer our own day, may be passed over in merciful silence. Poets give the public too much. Mr. Housman has followed the proud policy of giving too little.

When, in 1922, he put forth his second volume of verse, entitled *Last Poems,* there were some among his readers who re-
fused to take his implied threat seriously. This could not be
the end. Can a poet, even a successful one, hold his peace? But
those who knew the poet better realized at once that he would
rather die than publish another line of verse. His career as
poet was ended.

> To air the ditty,
> And to earth I.

Mr. Housman was sixty-three years old when that second volume, with its haughty preface, was published.

His poetry, as one begins to see it in perspective, reveals an
incredibly high level of worth. He is, par excellence, the poet
who has produced nothing poor. His poems all measure up to
a mark, and a mark set very high. He has no *juvenilia;* if he
has preserved his first sketches, the work of his 'prentice hand,
the world has been permitted to know nothing about them.
They have, no doubt, perished in flames, so that the secret of
his early training and practice may die with him. Hardly more
than a hundred poems in all have escaped his ruthlessness:
there are sixty-three poems in the first volume and forty-one
in the second. Only one of them extends to more than a hundred lines; and the first of them betrays the same skilled hand
that fashioned the last. All this gives the impression, as the
preface of 1922 explicitly asserts, that he has written only when
he has felt the goad of the muse. If so, his case is almost unique
in the annals of poetry, for the very greatest poets have clut-
tered up their volumes with the second-rate and the trivial, in
all honesty of conviction that they were still giving us of their
best. What scoffing Mephistopheles has pointed his critical fin-

ger to Housman's worthless lines, and caused them to be blotted out forever?

Perhaps the poet guessed that the public, even such readers as are concerned for the good of poetry, could not bear too much of him. Fastidious as he is, Mr. Housman is often repetitive. One may assert too often that youth and beauty must presently lie down in the lonely grave. For, as we might easily have too long a *Rubáiyát,* so we might speedily have too much of Mr. Housman and his lads. (The word "lad," by the way, occurs sixty-seven times in the first volume.) Terence, one remembers, is a performer on the flute, an instrument which, in a master's hand, utters a deliciously pure and limpid note, but one of which we presently grow weary. It is valued in proportion to its infrequency; so that we are not displeased when it is absorbed into larger harmonies.

He himself knows the folly of trying to prolong one's success unduly. With the bitter knowledge that comes only in middle age he realizes that the flowers from his garden may not always be "the wear." He is not the man to linger on the scene till his audience begins to melt away, but rather prefers to make an end before his admirers have realized their delight.

Characteristic of middle age, again, is the atmosphere of disillusion that prevails in his poetry. His are not the swift vicissitudes of joy and sorrow that mark a passionate youth; his moods are deep seated, never to be changed. He ceases not to sing of the land of lost content and happy highways where he cannot come again. In all the endless road we tread there's nothing but the night. These are the expressions of a man who has long since settled his philosophy and taken his stand. There are moments when he recalls the work of an earlier bard who also knew that the world can give us nothing equal in value to what it takes from us:

> For the sword outwears its sheath,
> And the soul wears out the breast,
> And the heart must pause to breathe,
> And Love itself have rest . . .

These lines were written when the author, Lord Byron, was nearing his twenty-ninth birthday, the age at which Housman, if we may trust his dates, wrote the first poem in *A Shropshire Lad*. The bulk of the volume was produced as late as 1895, when he was thirty-six, so that despite the perpetual assumption of youth, the sentiments are those of middle age. It is all reminiscential. About that there is nothing incredible: a poet may sing of "liquor, love, and fights" long after he has ceased to practice the arts mentioned.

It is not given to youth to speak with the professional skill of a Housman, whose manner, for all its apparent and engaging simplicity, results from a mature knowledge of the art of rhetoric (as it was once called, before modern colleges had brought it into disrepute), the French *éloquence*. Every phrase tells. His climax catches us unaware, like a blow upon the mouth, a blow carefully placed, delivered with full knowledge of its deadly force, by a professional hand. Not even in Browning can you find opening strains more blinding in their suddenness than,

> Shot? so quick, so clean an ending?
> Oh that was right, lad, that was brave.

It is only when we turn to his scholarly prose and particularly to his reviews of the publications of his rivals that we see how awful a power this may be when mercilessly applied. Professor Housman, who is professionally concerned with late Latin poetry, belongs to that extinct and evil school of reviewers, headed by Jeffrey and Brougham, who regarded the authors under their scrutiny as head-hunters do their captives. The wretched victims are neatly slaughtered, their heads cut off, and shrunken to the size and smiling contours of a wax doll's, and henceforth serve as trophies, proofs of the artist's skill—*sein Hand zu weisen*. There are those who admire this art, and if they wish to study it in detail may examine Professor Ferguson's essay, "The Belligerent Don." He cites an example (which I fear he admires) of a poor devil who had ventured to publish a translation of the elegies of Propertius, or *Cynthia,* as the first book of those somewhat artificial love poems used to be called. The translator modestly asked the reader's pardon for his "bald" rendering. Rash man! Professor Housman (a student of Horace, the poet who courteously referred to a rival as "stinking Maevius," and hoped that the ship on which he was putting forth to sea might go to the bottom) remarked in a review: " 'Scholars will pardon an attempt, however bald, to render into English these exquisite love poems.' Why? Those who have no Latin may pardon such an attempt, if they like bad verses better than silence; but I do not know why bald renderings of exquisite love poems should be pardoned by those who want no renderings at all."

Such blows are not unrelated to the art of the bully, nor are they unrelated to the art of the poet, as Horace and the Latin satirists have taught the Cambridge don. Those who enjoy British arrogance at its best may pursue this subject exhaustively in the classical and philological reviews to which Professor Housman has contributed.

I am not further concerned with all this than as it relates to the poet's very beautiful art, for, as I have said, the relation is there. The skill behind the savage prose and the force behind the poetry is the same shattering power. There is death in the words. In the simplest poems there is *passion* wound up to the intensest pitch. Take a poem like "The New Mistress." There is nothing really satirical about it, and a stanza chosen at random reads like one of the "Barrack Room Ballads":

> I will go where I am wanted, to a lady born and bred
> Who will dress me free for nothing in a uniform of red;
> She will not be sick to see me if I only keep it clean:
> I will go where I am wanted for a soldier of the Queen.

This obviously is Tommy Atkins speaking, but there is a subtlety in the poem to which Mr. Kipling never attains, a recurrent *motif* of sickness, which extends from the scornful sweetheart's "Oh, sick I am to see you," all the way to the final line, with its insistence upon the theme:

> And the enemies of England shall see me and be sick.

These verses are the product of a man who esteems workmanship as one of the best things to be found in poetry.

Housman is fond of writing about soldiers; but he is not forgetful of the bitterness of their lot:

> What evil luck soever
>   For me remains in store,
> 'Tis sure much finer fellows
>   Have fared much worse before.
>
> So here are things to think on
>   That ought to make me brave,

As I strap on for fighting
My sword that will not save.

It is natural that, among the elegies upon the dead who fell
in World War I, none is so powerful as Housman's, for he
realizes and stresses the unmitigated and abiding horror of it
all. No poem produced by that conflict sums up quite so well
the terror and the grim realism, not of the battlefield, but of
the cowering nations huddled watchfully behind their armies.

These, in the day when heaven was falling,
    The hour when earth's foundations fled,
Followed their mercenary calling,
    And took their wages, and are dead.

Their shoulders held the sky suspended;
    They stood, and earth's foundations stay;
What God abandoned, these defended,
    And saved the sum of things for pay.

An epitaph on an army of mercenaries! For sheer irony where
shall be found anything superior to "took their wages and are
dead"? Pathos, pity, and all the fine sentimentalities about
death on the field of glory drop out of mind and leave only the
stark finality of dying. Were a soldier's wages a shilling a day?
Yes, and death into the bargain. But compare it with the great
Greek epitaph on the soldiers who fell at Thermopylae, and
you see a difference: "Traveller, go tell the Lacedemonians that
here, obedient to their word, we lie." It is no less forceful, but it
is without bitterness.

Mr. Housman may idealize youth, but he never forgets its
temptation to violence and even to crime; and this may account, in some degree, for his strange preoccupation with

death by hanging. Nobody is likely to forget the pieces on this subject in *Last Poems,* or that horrible burlesque of the Crucifixion in the earlier volume, entitled "The Carpenter's Son," a poem that I prefer to pass without comment. It is not the poet's only satire on the Christian way of life.

> And if your hand or foot offend you,
>   Cut it off, lad, and be whole;
> But play the man, stand up and end you,
>   When your sickness is your soul.

This simple counsel and the oft-repeated theme that, though death is cruel, life is more cruel still, accounts, I suppose, for the adjective "pagan" that is so often applied to Housman's poetry; but this is hardly the correct term, for the pagan, properly so-called, is intensely religious in his way, "otherworldly" in truth; and to religion and its consolations Mr. Housman never makes a concession. Yet I cannot convince myself that such poems as "The Immortal Part," "The Carpenter's Son," and the ones on suicide are a considered message that it is better to enter into death than to endure the ignominy of life. I cannot even believe that they are intended to overthrow a consolatory religion and set up a grim and tight-lipped stoicism in its place. Mr. Housman does not use his poetry for "messages," and I doubt whether it is intended to influence our conduct in any way.

Poems of this sort have no ethical relations. If they were seriously intended as lessons of conduct, their author himself might reasonably be expected to apply them and make his stormy way to the grave. And we, the readers of this verse, can we be said really to have taken it to heart, unless we too play the man and set the pistol to our temple? However much we may admire this verse, our use of it is confined to the realm of the imagination, and never touches the more practical problems of conduct. If the function of a poem is merely to persuade the reader to mend his ways, or to adopt some high principle or noble standard of living, such verse is of secondary import, nothing more, indeed, than means to an end, means which may very properly be forgotten when the end is attained.

Take such a type of verse, for example, as the hymn. It releases within us certain emotions and instincts, memories and pieties which transcend poetry altogether and touch higher and more lasting concerns. A hymn which remains merely a poem, without influencing our walk and conversation, has not properly discharged its function. This is why it is impossible to evaluate hymns as literature; and the reason why poetry that is employed for propaganda can never be of a high order. This is what is wrong with the lyrics that William Morris wrote for the Socialist party of his day and what is wrong with such a thing as Mr. Auden's *Dance of Death,* because, effective as that satire on the modern world may be, it concludes with the triumph of Karl Marx and his young adherents. Like Mrs. Browning's *Bitter Cry of the Children,* it is dedicated to a cause and not to the muse.

The cause served by poetry is a peculiarly elevated one since it enriches the spirit by giving us vicarious experience and so enabling us to understand ways of life that are never to be ours. Hence it is that among the hosts who have loved the *Rubáiyát of Omar Khayyám,* few have tried to live by it, few have become winebibbers as a result of reading it, and fewer still have filled a drunkard's grave. We read Swinburne's most macabre ballads without sinking into degeneracy. We may read and admire *The City of Dreadful Night* without ourselves falling into melancholia, and may delight in the most sinister lyrics in *A Shropshire Lad* without the temptation to make away with ourselves or even to embrace the austerities of the Stoic school. But we are wiser and more experienced for having read these things, and have a larger conception of the incredible variety and intensity of human life.

No critic has been more insistent upon the non-ethical view of poetry than Mr. Housman himself, who has gone so far as to say that poetry is not the thing said but a way of saying it. His lecture on the "Name and Nature of Poetry," delivered at the University of Cambridge on May ninth, 1933, is a highly characteristic utterance, designed to annoy as well as to invigorate—a perfect irritant. "Meaning," he asserted, "is of the intellect, poetry is not." He affects to be wholly serious about this, and blandly announces that poetry is frequently the product of persons who have gone mad. He seems, throughout, to be thinking (like Poe) of poetry as consisting exclusively of brief lyric poems, what used to be called "ejaculations" or "effusions." Having told us that it is frequently "inadvisable" to draw the meaning out of such poems, he leaves us to decide for ourselves what to think of such vast works as the *Agamemnon* of Aeschylus, the *Oedipus* of Sophocles, the sixth book of the *Aeneid, King Lear,* and *The Divine Comedy.* If these things be not poetry, and, moreover, poetry at its most majestic, what are they henceforth to be deemed? If they are what the world has thought them hitherto, we must find a place for them in some poetic category, and we shall find it both possible and highly advisable to draw a meaning out of them. Such things, as Mr. Housman's own career reveals, are worth the attention of a lifetime.

But all this is from the point. The significant thing about

the lecture is its complete revelation of the personality of the author. It may be read with emotions similar in kind, if not in degree, to those awakened by his verse, and may serve, furthermore, as a commentary on it. Like his poetry the lecture is meant to startle and waylay. It succeeds in doing so. It proclaims that poetry is more physical than intellectual, that the seat of poetic sensation is the pit of the stomach, that poetry at its most intense makes the flesh creep and the hair of the head stand up. It is unwise to recite poetry to oneself while shaving. As for the act of creation, a certain deadening of the intellect is apparently desirable, and in Mr. Housman's case, at least in the days of *A Shropshire Lad,* the poet before beginning to compose drank a pint of beer at luncheon, as a "sedative to the brain."

Those may take this seriously who can. For my part, I cannot forget Housman's besetting temptation to jostle the ark of the covenant. I cannot forget that he must be aware of the activity in Cambridge of Mr. I. A. Richards and his young school. I can imagine his delight in telling the dons and the bluestockings in his audience how he had answered a foolish American who had asked him for a definition of poetry. (An English lecturer can always get a laugh by girding at Americans.) Housman replied that one could no more define poetry than a terrier can define a rat, but that he thought both recognized the object by the symptoms which it provokes in us. In which there is of course something deliciously unregenerate, something pungent and slightly sulphurous, highly amusing and quite unacceptable.

There is nothing in the lecture to indicate any waning of the poet's powers, so that the reader cannot but wish that instead of this vigorous and provocative lecture, we might have had another slender volume of perfect and provocative verse. But this is to cry for the moon. Housman has spoken eloquent words about the exhaustion that ensues for the poet upon the completion of his work: "I can no longer expect to be revisited by the continuous excitement under which . . . I wrote the greater part of my other book [*A Shropshire Lad*], nor indeed could I well sustain it if it came."

That is his *apologia*. He has bidden us farewell in one of the most beautiful "variations on a theme" that has ever been wrought in English:

> We'll to the woods no more,
> The laurels all are cut,
> The bowers are bare of bay
> That once the Muses wore;
> The year draws in the day
> And soon will evening shut:
> The laurels all are cut,
> We'll to the woods no more.
> Oh we'll no more, no more
> To the leafy woods away,
> To the high wild woods of laurel
> And the bowers of bay no more.

Here is that power to pierce the breast with unutterable emotion of which Mr. Housman lectured so eloquently, and which he would, rather rashly, hold to be the sole and complete mark of poetry.

Whether it be so or not is a question that does not concern us here: if not the highest power possessed by poets, it is certainly among the highest. It is one which we shall, I think, seek in vain among other living poets in England. Who, now that Mr. Housman has fallen silent, stabs the heart with the sudden and unforgettable word? Who speaks the word that conquers and controls the breast, and gives utterance to the deepest emotions of the spirit, and so becomes a partner in the will of the Creator? Mr. Kipling has remarkable gifts—gifts which at the moment are perhaps too lightly esteemed—but this has never been reckoned among them. The laureate has depended upon other means to touch the emotions and to hold the interest. The younger poets are preoccupied with their own emotions and their exciting program, and are probably unaware that the public has a heart to stab.

Although Mr. Housman has condemned himself to silence, he has not been without his active influence upon the literary world. He has remained a symbol of sanity and intelligibility, and has reminded us that a poet may have a larger audience than his own narrow circle of personal friends. The enduring steadiness of his poetic reputation has served as a commentary on the rise and fall of the paltry poetic fashions of the day. As a poet he has displayed a becoming modesty in strange contrast to his native arrogance. He has never pandered to the public taste or solicited the discipleship of poets; but he has kept alive the notion that a poet has a profession to learn and a duty to fulfil. His pride in his craft has been contagious. Meanwhile he has been content to be Professor of Latin and an authority on Manilius. His activity in this chosen field he has been pleased to describe as his "proper job"; posterity will remember him for a "job" of a very different kind, but one discharged with no less professional skill.

This essay was written in 1935 at the request of the editors of *The Yale Review*. In it I naturally expressed my admiration for the high standard of excellence which the poet had imposed upon himself. The ability to distinguish between one's best work and that which, though produced with as much care and conviction as the rest, nevertheless stubbornly remains inferior, is the rarest of all a poet's endowments. He cannot bring himself to destroy that of which he had once such high hopes. Housman died in 1936, and it was then discovered that he had left to his younger brother, Laurence, the right to publish or destroy such verse as remained behind in manuscript. The executor was enjoined not to print anything that would in any way injure the reputation so carefully built up in *A Shropshire Lad* and *Last Poems*. The manuscript of this unpublished verse I had the privilege of reading in the summer of 1936, and I fervently prayed for its destruction. It contained six poems which might safely have been added to the "canon" of Housman's poetic work, though to have withheld them would not in any way have lowered it. Mr. Laurence Housman, not unnaturally, gave a very loose interpretation to the restriction which his brother had laid upon him, for he had not only his brother's reputation as poet to think of, but his own reputation as critic. The result was that the public was permitted to see a large amount of second-rate material. Forty-eight pieces were added in *More Poems,* 1936, and thirty-one in *A. E. H.,* 1937; the poet himself had printed but one hundred and four in all. One could now peruse such mournful stuff as

> From the wash the laundress sends
> My collars home with ravelled ends,

and

> They're taking him to prison for the colour of his hair.

Well, we now know that the Parian finish of Housman's poems was the result of an anxious attention and a stern self-discipline, and not an inexplicable gift from on high. And the lesson is clear enough. If a poet desires to suppress what he deems unworthy, he would do well to destroy it himself and not leave the task to one less intimately concerned.

XI

Trollope

IT is natural that an essay on Trollope should begin with statistics. To forget his voluminousness is like ignoring the extent of the ocean or the height of Mount Everest. He, like many of the greatest authors—Shakespeare, Boccaccio, Chaucer, Sophocles—is remarkable partly for having written so much. In an age of great novelists, he surpassed them all in output. His full-length novels, some forty-seven in number, exceed the total number of Dickens', Thackeray's, and George Eliot's combined. If we reckon volumes of short stories and books of travel, he produced twice as much as Walter Scott. He requires, in one's library, not a capacious shelf but an entire bookcase.

Of this fecundity the author was obviously proud. As everybody knows, he imposed upon himself a rigorous system of daily composition with which nothing was permitted to interfere. He never waited for inspiration. He wrote in railway trains and on shipboard. He wrote when physically and mentally uncomfortable, and even when seasick. At one time he began work at 5.30 A.M., wrote with his watch on the table before him, and exacted from himself 250 words every quarter of an hour. Henry James, in his pleasant essay on Trollope, bears testimony to this habit: "It was once the fortune of the author of these lines to cross the Atlantic in his [Trollope's] company, and he has never forgotten the magnificent example of plain persistence that it was in the power of the eminent novelist to give on that occasion. The season was unpropitious, the vessel overcrowded, the voyage detestable; but Trollope shut himself up in his cabin every morning . . . for communion with the muse."

He boasted that he could have produced three novels in three volumes each in the course of a year, had he been so disposed. There was a smooth, rapid stream of publication for a quarter of a century, from 1857 to 1882, which ended only with his death, when he left behind him two complete novels—*Mr. Scarborough's Family* (an excellent tale) and *An Old Man's Love*—an unfinished Irish story, *The Land Leaguers,* and an *Autobiography* in two volumes. This amazing and unbroken productivity was not begun till the author had entered his thirty-third year, and he had no great success till he was past forty. One result of this late beginning is that he appears, even at first, in full maturity. He had made no false starts. *The Macdermots of Ballycloran,* his earliest novel, contains little of the charm which was later to be associated with his name; but there is no trace in it of a 'prentice hand. It is profoundly depressing, but well written and cleverly constructed. It holds the attention of the horrified reader to the end. The author rightly regarded the plot of *The Macdermots* as the equal of any that he constructed.

But there is more significance in Trollope's inexhaustible abundance than mere quantity. Strangely enough, it contributes in a way to his popularity, for it means that those who love his work can go on reading him forever. By the time you have read forty of his stories, you are ready to begin again. Dickens, though less extensive, has for his partisans something of the same appeal.

Moreover, Trollope, like Tintoretto, requires a huge canvas. He is not given to microscopic detail, reconsideration, or altered approach. He has so much to say that he not only fills the canvas, but, like Zola, expands his novels into series. His two great examples of continued narrative, the "cathedral series" and the "parliamentary series," are the greatest specimens of their kind in the English language, unless, indeed, Galsworthy has surpassed them. Again, Trollope sees man in society, as an individual in a group. He seldom concerns himself with the solitary or the picaro. There is no Barry Lyndon or Peregrine Pickle in the vast panorama of his work. Nor does he explore the hidden recesses of the mind, like Joseph Conrad, passing from chamber to inner chamber, till he reaches the very arcana of the soul. He thought George Eliot too analytical. To this general assertion, exception must be made of *He Knew He Was Right,* a story of the development of insanity out of the stubborn pride of a man unable to conceive of himself as being in the wrong.

If Trollope took a pardonable pride in his incredible fertility, he was forced to pay a penalty for being fool enough to tell about it. The *Autobiography,* in which his rigorous methods were disclosed to the public, appeared in 1883, and was read with consternation by a generation which had come to delight in subtler standards and a more esoteric manner. It was an age in which much was heard about the *mot juste* and the figured harmony of prose. The novelists of the new school took an obvious delight in leading the reader a chase. It became the custom to speak slightingly of the reader's concern with mere "story," and to smile at the old-fashioned desire for a happy ending. To the newer generation Trollope was a writer who did not take his art seriously. Henry James, in his most telling fashion, remarked that "the writing of novels had ended by becoming with him a perceptibly mechanical process." He could turn out fiction by the yard, as though engaged in operating a machine. The very names of his characters betrayed his superficiality. Dr. Fillgrave and Mr. Quiverful (so inferior to the more suggestive names used by Thackeray) were laughed at, and even his limpid style did not escape scorn. Had he not praised Thackeray for the wrong thing by remarking, "The reader without labor knows what he means, and knows all he means"? Perfect communion between author and reader was no longer attempted by the former nor desired by the latter. To a generation beginning to admire Meredith, he still harped on the importance of clarity. He thought George Eliot "struggled too hard." "She lacked ease," he said.

But perhaps Trollope's perfect clarity and unpretentiousness may, in his own case, prove to be a saving grace, in that this very lack of manner keeps him from becoming antiquated. His style does not "date," like that of many of his contemporaries. It has no spot of decay, but has kept sweet as the decades have passed.

Other features of the novelist's art are dismissed by Trollope in his *Autobiography* with a similar unconcern. Novel writing all seems—or is made to seem—incredibly easy. Mere plot never troubled him, and he has therefore been accused of formlessness. Although none of his works is remarkable for a classic roundness, for finish and economy of means, I cannot feel that this charge is apposite. He is guided only by what he conceives to be the reader's desire. He will not continue a story after the reader's interest has lapsed. He never leaves the reader guessing or stops the story midway because life is without clear and fixed terminations.

There are times when he overloads his novel with material that may fairly be called extraneous. The satiric passages in

The Warden are an ugly blot on the perfection of a story which, for once, is admirably constructed. One can forgive a failure to appreciate the buoyant, Brobdingnagian manner of Dickens, which Trollope never properly esteemed, but is at a loss to understand why he should wish to devote so many scornful paragraphs to him as "Mr. Sentiment," and even to ridicule two of his well-known characters, Mr. Buckett and Mrs. Gamp. The attack adds nothing to the story, and the whole incident (if such it may be called) could have been excised by the stroke of a pen. The caricature of Carlyle as Dr. Pessimist Anticant, which includes a kind of parody of *Past and Present,* is even worse. It is ill natured and long drawn out, and is, unhappily, not clever. And there are other things in the novels that could be spared. Many readers—particularly Americans—find the chapters devoted to fox hunting a weariness to the mind, and others are repelled by the political issues of the parliamentary series; but, considering the vast extent of Trollope's work, it is surprising how little one is tempted to skip and how little one can omit without loss.

But all these are matters of secondary importance. Trollope himself declared that the first duty of a novelist was to have a story to tell, and of this principle he was a scrupulous observer. Although he was indifferent to that smoothness and sequence of events which are found in the great masterpieces of plot, he was careful enough of the main problem, careful, that is, to lend a continuous interest to it. The presence of this feature may generally be detected by the question that is uppermost in the reader's mind, and two of Trollope's titles plainly reveal it, *Can You Forgive Her?* and *Is He Popinjoy?* In the latter the recurrent question, "Is the Italian baby who was born abroad, in circumstances that cannot be investigated, the real heir to the name or is he illegitimate?" holds the entire story together and dominates the reader's attention throughout. And thus it is in other books. Can John Eames win the hand of Lily Dale? Did Lady Mason forge the codicil to her dying husband's will? Where did Mr. Crawley get the check which caused all the trouble in *The Last Chronicle of Barset?* In *Cousin Henry,* where is the missing will? Was Mr. Scarborough's eldest son really illegitimate, and if not, what was his father's motive in declaring him to be so? (A single sentence on the first page of *Mr. Scarborough's Family* initiates this interest: "The world has not yet forgotten the intensity of the feeling which existed when old Mr. Scarborough declared that his well-known eldest son was not legitimate.") It is such questions as these that lead the reader on from chapter to thrilling chapter; and such problems may surely be said to constitute plot, if such a thing as plot there be.

Trollope never belittled the importance in fiction of exciting incidents. He defends sensationalism in his *Autobiography,* and contends that a good novel should be both realistic and sensational, and "in the highest degree." "If a novel fail in either," he adds, "there is a failure in art." People who think of Trollope as drab and rather unexciting do not sufficiently reckon with this feature of his work. George Vavasor tries to kill his rival, John Grey, and comes very near doing so; Lady Mason is brought into court, and tried for perjury; the Reverend Mark Robarts' house is invaded by the sheriff's officers; Phineas Finn is tried for murder; and Sir Henry Harcourt, the successful and admired, commits suicide. Such a list could be indefinitely prolonged. But Trollope was not so foolish as to suppose that incidents like these were all-sufficient. Who cares about wills or diamonds or questions of legitimacy unless he is concerned for the persons whose lives are to be made or ruined by the disclosure of the truth? And, therefore, the author was primarily concerned with "realism," in that he was careful first to waken the reader's sympathy for the man or woman involved. In certain stories, as, for example, in *The Warden,* the question before us is so simple as to seem almost trifling unless the reader is deeply moved for the hero's peace of mind. An elderly clergyman, precentor in Barchester Cathedral, is made to debate with himself whether his modest post as warden of Hiram's Hospital is consistent with a rigorous ideal of honesty. Can he continue to hold it undisturbed by the disquieting thought that it is a mere sinecure? His final surrender and resignation of the wardenship are made as thrilling as a shipwreck, but only because the reader has first learned to love the patient, Christian fortitude of the man. We should be equally concerned if anything were to happen to his precious violoncello. Among Trollope's countless portraits, there is no more admirable, no more appealing and lovable man than this aged musician, who has outlived all personal ambition and uneasy jealousy, and has now no other desire than to live a simple and godly life. The account of his death is one of the most moving chapters ever written by a novelist.

Or take the story of Lizzie Eustace—the fascinating and unscrupulous adventuress, who has the aims of Becky Sharp without her cleverness. I doubt whether any woman can read her story with enjoyment, but I am confident that any man will fall at moments under her spell and, for the time being, wish her well in her mean little plot. If one is not amused by her shifts and her shameful deceit, he will, of course, close the book and read no more, since all interest in what becomes of the jewels will have declined long since. I am confident that the author himself had a kind of inverted sympathy with her and her schemes. There is in her the abiding interest of the adventuress.

And yet Lizzie is but a pale creature compared with her radiant predecessor, "Madeline Vesey Neroni, nata Stanhope." The daughter of Dr. Stanhope, of the cathedral chapter (now returned to Barchester close after a long period of non-residence), she has been reared, married, and widowed in Italy, and has devised for herself the surprising nomenclature used above. She is a cripple, condemned to pass her life lying on a sofa, but her spirit and her beauty enable her to use it as a throne, from which she proceeds to fascinate the Reverend Mr. Slope and other men of Barchester. No reader of *Barchester Towers* will forget her apparition at Mrs. Proudie's reception in the Bishop's palace. Her sofa is wheeled into the crowded assembly, and she is seen lying on her couch arrayed in white velvet—

without any other garniture than rich white lace worked with pearls across her bosom and the same round the armlets of her dress. Across her brow she wore a band of red velvet, on the centre of which shone a magnificent Cupid in mosaic. . . . On the one arm which her position required her to expose she wore three magnificent bracelets each of different stones. Beneath her on the sofa and over the cushion and head of it was spread a crimson silk mantle or shawl which went under her whole body and concealed her feet. Dressed as she was and looking as she did, so beautiful yet so motionless, . . . with that lovely head, and those large bold bright staring eyes, it was impossible that either man or woman should do other than look at her.

It was on this occasion that the wheel of her sofa came in contact with the lace train of Mrs. Proudie's gown: "Gathers were heard to go, stitches to crack, plaits to fly open, flounces were seen to fall, and breadths to expose themselves;—and a long ruin of rent lace disfigured the carpet, and still clung to the vile wheel on which the sofa moved!" But Madeline Vesey Neroni lies in Olympian beauty gazing upon it all with a serene composure in which one may detect a mild amusement. So might a recumbent goddess have gazed on some earthly frivolity far beneath her. Madeline is an impostor, but she is brilliant and indomitable, and a male reader may find it in his heart to wish her well.

As Trollope has made the base motives of Lizzie and Madeline amusing, so he has the power, even more remarkable, of lending an air of authenticity and importance to the unpleasant. He wrote many unpleasant stories, but somehow the reading of them is not unpleasant. I can, I think, read them all with pleasure, except the horrible psychological study, remorselessly pursued to its conclusion in madness—*He Knew He Was Right*. Of this novel, the author wrote in his *Autobiography,* "It was my purpose to create sympathy for the unfortunate man, who, while endeavouring to do his duty to all around him, should be led constantly astray by his unwillingness to submit his own judgment to the opinion of others. . . . I look upon the story as being nearly altogether bad." In this stricture every reader will, I think, heartily concur.

But I do not find *The Bertrams* unpleasant, though the author himself did, and though the events are, in all conscience, painful enough. There are three unhappy love affairs, and though two of the couples are brought together at the end, there is but little delight in the reader's heart. Youth is revealed in its least attractive moods, harsh, sullen, proud, stubborn, and selfish. Age is even more relentlessly depicted. Old Mr. Bertram, who has an important part in the complication of the story, is dismissed by the author as a bad man, whose money was his god. One could believe that at this period in his life, Trollope cherished a grudge against old age, for the disagreeable Mr. Bertram is duplicated in Lord Stapledean, a detestable ogre without a redeeming trait. Nor is the fair sex spared. Mrs. Wilkinson, widow of a vicar, is a feeble reflection of Mrs. Proudie and a pathetic fool as well, who is actually made to refer to herself as in charge of the parish of her late husband, though her son has succeeded to the post. There is, moreover, a hateful old cat, a Mrs. Reake of Rissbury, who spits venom in her every sentence; but she somehow remains credible. And there is a witch of hell who reviles her partner at whist until she drives her mad. These, and the two widows (if such they be) whom young Bertram and Wilkinson meet on their voyage from Alexandria, present a view of womankind which is by no means flattering. The story is brought to an end by the suicide of Sir Henry Harcourt, for whose degeneracy and fall no exculpatory word can be found.

All this makes the author's assertion that he should wish a serene gratification to flow from his pages seem almost ironical. Why, then, is one justified in saying that *The Bertrams,* and even *Marion Fay* and *Sir Harry Hotspur,* may be read with a certain pleasure? What is the explanation of that vivid warming of the heart that one feels from time to time as one reads on? Is it not due to the association with the author himself, a man worldly-wise, yet kindly and, above all, fair-minded? Not even Henry Fielding associates with his readers on more agreeable terms. We do not care to lose ourselves wholly in the story, for we remember that Trollope is with us as a kind of chorus. This pleasant art he learned, it may be, from Thackeray, the god of his idolatry. But in Trollope there is none of Thackeray's pretension, no condescending to his characters, many of whom he frankly adores. He is forever saying what can be brought forward in extenuation of their actions; and at last the reader comes to feel that he would want for himself no more sympathetic and indulgent advocate.

Sometimes, to be sure, the author says too much. There are moments when he *will* be talking, though the reader wishes he would get on with the story. He insists on telling us about his travels. *Can You Forgive Her?* reflects two visits to Switzerland. *The Bertrams* is full of his travels to the Near East and the Holy Land. He must vent his feelings about Jerusalem and Alexandria, and boast that an Englishman can thrash an Arab. He confesses that he has difficulty in repressing the desire to write a book about Malta.

But when Trollope speaks to us out of the depths of his practical and kindly wisdom, no devoted reader will fail to give him a hearing. There is nothing very original or subversive in his opinions, but they are a kind of gracious common sense issuing from a warm heart and a large sympathy. In *Framley Parsonage* he has this to say of the grief felt by Lucy Robarts on the death of her father: "Nobody had yet spoken to her about her father since she had been at Framley. It had been as though the subject were a forbidden one. And how frequently is this the case! When those we love are dead, our friends dread to mention them, though to us who are bereaved no subject would be so pleasant as their names. But we rarely understand how to treat our own sorrow or those of others." There is nothing profound here, only good counsel of what may be called the middle sort, but for that very reason all the more important, for we are seldom in a mood—and never in the hour of bereavement—to receive and apply truths of the sublimer kind.

We have no leisure from our grief to debate their validity or meditate on their usefulness. The commonplaceness of Trollope's opinions such as the above is the source of their value to thousands who could have given no ear to the consolations of philosophy.

In *Orley Farm,* when Lady Mason has been crushed to earth by the confession of her guilt, the words spoken by Mrs. Orme to comfort her have no originality at all, and the author himself concedes that Mrs. Orme was not strong-minded. "This lady took her to her heart again and promised in her ear, with low sweet words of consolation, that they should still be friends. I cannot say that Mrs. Orme was right. That she was weak-minded I feel nearly certain. But perhaps this weakness of mind may never be brought against her to her injury, either in this world or in the next."

"Sentimentality," cries the reader, and such no doubt it is; but so is Portia's speech on mercy in *The Merchant of Venice,* and so, for that matter, is the whole doctrine of forgiveness, the motive for which springs out of the emotions with slight aid from ratiocination. It might be argued, I suppose, that such sentimentality is rational in some subtle respect, but that is not Trollope's way. He has none of George Eliot's habit of viewing such matters in a philosophical light. His views are set forth not as admonitions or newly discovered truths but as the natural sunshine of life. He reflects ordinary existence with such fidelity that his remarks never seem inopportune or dragged in to mend our morals or our daily conduct. Perhaps no subtler praise can be given than to call him companionable. He never sets himself up as arbiter or pretends to be wiser than we; but he is charitable and broad-minded, and it is a privilege to be with him.

Trollope never used his art to promote a particular reform or to bring a current scandal to public attention. He neither interrupted nor deflected the course of fiction in his own day, for he had no revolutionary theories or mannerisms, so that of all the great Victorian novelists, he is the most engaging because of his very simplicity. He was content to be a storyteller and an entertainer, and saw no reason to blush for his profession, which he sometimes mischievously referred to as a trade. His aim was to depict life as he saw it all about him, "enlivened by humour and sweetened by pathos," crowding his canvas with figures, and ranging with ease from the vulgar to the noble, from the commonplace to the sensational, from the streetwalker to the duchess, from a tout at the race course to the chancellor on the woolsack. He had a natural love of human beings, and his novels are a radiant reflection of it. These are the qualities that made him popular in his own generation; these are the qualities, construed as weaknesses, which clouded his reputation for a quarter of a century after his death, when he was reckoned among those who, even in their lifetime, had written themselves out, and were doomed to oblivion. And these are the very qualities which have enabled him in our own day to renew his strength, and demonstrate once again his happy skill in entertaining a host of readers.

XII

Hand and Soul *

An Address delivered to the Graduating Class of the Yale School of the Fine Arts. June 12, 1941.

I MUST confess quite freely that I feel somewhat like an intruder on this occasion. "What," you may properly inquire, "has a mere literary critic to say—what, indeed, will he dare to say—about the lovely arts to the study and creation of which this School is dedicated?" You work with brilliant light and flowing line and prismatic colors, and you are perpetually and professionally concerned with beauty. It is the world in which you live. Very different is the province in which the literary man has his being. Even in that humble and outlying suburb of literary criticism, where I sojourn, there is nothing parallel to the experience of the plastic artist. You are craftsmen. I am not. You who have now completed your training here are, I assume, all in some degree skillful of hand, with practiced control of the muscles, and with thoughts or images to impress upon stone or canvas or etched plate or engraved block; whereas any literary man is engaged in a secret and invisible struggle far within the chambers of the mind. His medium is the elusive word, and it is a medium that often seems to him to be worn with age and tarnished with use, yet into this he must contrive to force his meaning. It is all vague and

* This title was filched, deliberately, from D. G. Rossetti.

formless compared with the experience of the artist who has the joy of seeing a *thing* grow under his hand. In that creative process I am wholly inexperienced. I am like a child who stands staring at a painter who has set up his easel in the fields, or like one of those visitors to the great hall on Treasure Island, where one could watch a man frescoing a wall or a sculptor hacking a heroic figure out of wood or marble. I love the swift sure stroke of the artist's hand.

I confess that I am envious of that skill of hand. It is something visible, something demonstrable, something, if I may venture the assertion, that can be talked about. I recall that great painters have been more disposed to boast of their manual skill than of their inspiration, and that they often expect their pupils, their admirers, and their critics to seek for evidence of their genius in sketches and drawings and first conceptions rather than in finished works. Ruskin long ago pointed out the significance of the old story of Giotto's circle, drawn freehand. Such is the passion for technical perfection which the artist feels; and I have noticed that the severest criticism that one painter passes upon another is that "he cannot draw," or that "he has no sense of color," as though it were quite damnable enough to assert so much and no more.

Because of my love of this manual skill, I am fond of the Dutch School. They have so obviously learned their job. They know their *métier,* as the French say. And among the painters of the Dutch School, my favorites are those lesser masters who seem content wherever they turn, and are not forever running about looking for inspiration or novelty. They revere what they know and bestow upon the representation of the familiar the transfiguring light of their technical skill. They delight in flowers and insects and vegetables and raw meat, and their

ugly whitewashed churches, and the long flat sweep of the
Dutch countryside, with a few acres of linen bleaching in the
sun—good "Holland of eight shillings an ell," as Shakespeare
called it. No phase of their life is too humble and no object too
common or unclean to waken the artist's passion to observe, to
record, and to interpret. I have heard many persons question
the inspiration of these little masters, who are the great masters of still life, but I have never heard anybody disparage
their drawing. Van Huysum with his vase of flowers, De Heem
with his musical instruments and oyster shells and lemon peel,
Kalb with his rugs and his blue china, and Van der Heyden
eternally at work in village streets—all these had the root of
the matter in them, for they knew how to paint.

I recall a little picture in the Amsterdam gallery which has
long been a favorite of mine because of its incredible combina-
tion of perfect draftsmanship with utter commonplaceness and
modesty of appeal. The painter was Adrian Coorte, and the picture shows three or four stalks of asparagus, tied together in
a bunch and lying on a white dish. That is all. And yet . . .

At this point I seem to hear the derisive word "representa-
tional" whispered in protest, for some of you have already begun to think it odd that I should come here to speak on so
antiquated a theme as imitative painting. As a matter of fact,
I plead not guilty to the charge. I assent to the doctrine that in
a true work of art there is something that no camera can catch,
and that even Shakespeare's famous advice to actors to hold
the mirror up to nature is insufficient as making no reference to
the personality of the artist. There is an inimitable something
in any great work of art that springs from the soul of the
artist. Indeed, I regard this as the ultimate truth about those
humbler Dutch masters of whom I have spoken. I am aware

that Van Huysum sheds a glory over a vase of flowers that I could never detect for myself, even if I could assemble the scores of blossoms that he puts in; and I know very well that, even had I been present when Van der Heyden was painting his village street, I should have failed to find the beauty that he discovered there. "The seeing eye is still the loving eye."

We know now that the traditional "grand style" (like the charm of the Dutch School) issues not from the subject chosen, but from the soul of the artist operating upon it and creating a new splendor. The artist's hand embodies and interprets the unseen thing in his imagination, where the form of the original may be superseded; and hence arises that elusiveness, that inexplicable something in all true works of art, which vitiates the critic's analysis, and too often brings forth angry remonstrances from the indignant artist. He seems to be forever saying, "I have done my work; now make of it what you can." When we consider the hasty fashion in which people approach, glance at, and dismiss the works of the artist, there is nothing very churlish in this manner. For the thing that the artist, be he sculptor, painter, or architect, is striving to express is hidden far within the *penetralia* of his spirit; the object with which he is immediately concerned is but the point of departure. "The beauty of which we are in quest is general and intellectual; it is an idea that subsists only in the mind; the sight never beheld it, nor has the hand expressed it; it is an idea residing in the breast of the artist, which he is always labouring to impart, and which he dies at last without imparting." These are the words of Reynolds, addressed to artists, not primarily to the public, though they were later given to the public. To the word "impart" I invite your special attention. The speaker intimates that an artist is striving to *give* us something, to communicate with us; and so the whole process becomes a kind of communion between the artist (who gives) and the layman (who receives). The time will never come when the artist will find no satisfaction in the impression he makes upon the public mind. It is all stupid nonsense to assert that an artist paints or carves or builds only to please himself or to express his own creative impulse. A Crusoe, no matter how highly endowed, will paint no pictures and carve no statues while on his desert island, unless he knows that he can take them with him when his long exile is ended and he returns to the society of his fellows. Crusoe would erect no fair dwelling house for himself and no soaring temple for the honor of his God, unless he were confident that a posterity were to follow him in his island, to use and enjoy the beautiful works of his hand and soul. Nay, would not their very beauty have risen out of his desire to communicate with his fellows? Wanting a public, he would want also the creative impulse. All that the artist makes is, in reality, done for posterity; and that is not very different from asserting that it is done for you and me and for the great stupid public.

If, then, the greatness of all art is finally tested by the frame of mind into which it plunges the layman, it must, I think, be admitted, even by the most advanced and emancipated practitioners among us, that the relations between the artist and the layman have not, during the past quarter century, been at all satisfactory. Listen to the words of a contemporary though anonymous critic. I know only that it is an Englishman who speaks, and that he has the present world crisis uppermost in mind:

There have been ominous signs of an almost universal fatigue of the spirit, varying in different lands. . . . Many of us, in sheer intellectual laziness, were falling into a premature senility, contented with ready-made entertainments of all kinds that required no personal exertion from ourselves. . . . Impatient of those entertainments and studies that demand mental alertness and cooperation, [many were] rusting into [a] condition of [mere] receptivity.

"Intellectual laziness," "rusting," "senility," these are severe indictments; but the attack, insofar as it may be called such, is, you notice, directed *not* at the artist but at the general public. It is a diagnosis. It finds the cause of our present unhappy condition in our apathy, in our tendency to decline into mere receptivity, and to think of works of art as existing merely to provide us with entertainment in our leisure hours or our sluggish moods. The public wants, of course, like the great hungry creature it is, to be pampered. But if artists pamper the public, the public will, like children, expect to be pampered more and more. They are like children whom a grown-up is amusing. "Do it again," they say. And you will do it again till the child's imagination wanders to something else. Now no one can blame the artist for resenting such an attitude; and I can readily understand that the strange new manner so prevalent in art today reflects a pardonable disdain for persons too apathetic to spend the time and effort necessary to master the idiom in which the artist addresses us.

For the public this rift between the artist and the layman is deplorable in the extreme, for it is fraught with peril on both sides. It is dangerous for the public because it is always more dangerous to receive than to give; and to sink into a state in which one asks only for amusement, and in the end only for the satisfaction of the appetites. That such a result is inevitable will be doubted only by those who have never visited a night club, and witnessed the frame of mind common among its habitués.

Just what the artist is to do about all this I do not venture to say, nor should I make any deep impression on you if I did. You would be scornfully amused at my audacity; but perhaps, speaking on behalf of the great childish public, I may be permitted to remark that it would be a happy thing for all if there were somewhat more coöperation between the artist and the layman, for the world's need of the artist is rapidly becoming acute, and it is to be hoped that some sort of truce may be negotiated, or the plight of the artist will also presently be acute. The standards that have prevailed in the last three decades are about to fall; the one thing that we can be certain of is that the present style will change, and probably change radically. And I suspect that that artist will travel farthest who shall have most faith in mankind, conceiving of man not merely as a sensual brute tearing his brother to pieces in the bloody slime, and not merely as a mechanized robot in a vast machine, and, above all, not merely a bewildered businessman wondering what the government and the unions are going to do next, but as an anomalous creature, who feels two natures struggling within him, moving about in a world in which he never feels quite at home, teased with "thoughts beyond the reaches of his soul"—a being *"rudely* great," to be sure, but still with the hallmark of a master workman upon him, a being capable of growth and, on the whole, worth saving.

I conceive of the artist as a person specially commissioned to lead and to invigorate this strange spirit, this creature who sinks so easily into the slough of animalism, and to lift him to a realization of his own dignity. Artists of one kind or another man *must* have. He cannot exist without the architect, for he must have shelter for his mate and children, and he readily takes a pride in his dwelling place, and enjoys seeing it become, in some fashion, expressive of his personality and of his aspirations. And since this hulking creature, like any other child, will look at pictures all day long, the painter may hope to get his attention where a poet or even a storyteller would fail; for the painter appeals to the eye, and by means of this, the most precious of the five senses, he may touch the creature's emotions and may influence his will.

This is the task that awaits the artist, and one hopes that its accomplishment may not be long delayed. It is a task worthy of the best spirit among us—one who is no slave to the paltry notion that works of art are a mere reflection of the age in which they are produced. The truly great artist is one who sets his course *away* from the temper of the age, and by resisting it points it in a new direction:

> Ever the poet from the land
> Steers his bark and trims his sail,
> Right out to sea his courses stand,
> New worlds to find in pinnace frail.

At no time in human history, perhaps, has there been so great a need for this creative artist—not only because of that lethargic mood into which the public has sunk, but also because of the dreadful fact that each day that passes reveals the progressive impoverishment of the world, as great buildings, statues, and pictures are taken from us forever. The testing of the next generation—your generation—will be of its ability to restore a portion of the splendor that has been lost. That you will record something more than the fears and disillusions which have been our daily fare, we may permit ourselves to hope; that you will strike out something to console us and to outlive the tragedy through which we are passing can occur only if you shall have faith in the dignity of man, whom you serve, and in the spark of eternal fire that is at the heart of him.

XIII

Sitter and Portrait*

OF all the vices to which poor human nature is prone, none surely is more disagreeable than self-consciousness or *mauvaise honte*. It is at once a folly and the punishment of folly, since it makes the victim hateful to himself and a spectacle to others. Whatever it be, nothing generates it so promptly as sitting for one's picture. A "sitter" has delivered himself over to the inquisitor; he is "on trial," and has no appeal to a higher court. If the painter's view of him is mortifying, there is nothing to be done about it. The sitter can never hope to answer the artist back, for the artist has always a ready retort—"Such is the way you look to me."

If the painter, with sly courtesy, asks your opinion, your comment, however diffidently expressed, your modest appeal for amelioration at one point or for merciful softening of a line or shadow at another, only sinks you deeper into the quicksand of your own self-conceit and your ill-concealed desire to appear handsomer or cleverer than you are.

Nor does the painter's explanation that he is not so much recording a likeness as interpreting a character put a sitter at his ease. This only makes matters worse, for it announces the painter's right to manipulate the evidence before him. It may

---

* The natural title for this essay would seem to be "On Sitting for One's Portrait," but that happy title has already been used by Hazlitt, with whom one would not willingly challenge comparison.

result very happily if the painter enjoys what he is doing; but what, oh what, will happen when he grows weary or disgusted with the work to which he has set his hand? What will the painter (as interpreter) do when the horrible realization steals over him that his sitter is a fool or worse, and certainly not worth all this study and fuss?

What wonder if, at such a crisis, a portraitist should succumb to the temptation to tell more than actually meets his eye, should hint at what the sitter is so anxiously attempting to hide, and satirize or even caricature the person before him. What fun to deflate the ridiculous creature! What subtle pleasure (and what deadly sin) to paint that hidden folly, and yet, at the same moment, somehow delight the victim, so that he shall share in the dirty work!

What a disastrous record of one's folly and commonplaceness a portrait can be!—like that awful series of portraits of the entire Wertheimer family (the tribe of Ashur) in which Mr. Sargent ministered to the vanity of the founder. And there is Mr. Augustus John (of the Academy), who can make a portrait as libelous as one of Mr. Lytton Strachey's brief biographies. But what is the miserable sitter to expect? He has delivered himself over. *Sitters must be content.* Their dissatisfaction, if they are fool enough to give it utterance, is a fitting punishment for their presumption in sitting at all.

The artist can, of course, be the very opposite of a satirist and adopt the way of mercy. A lucky sitter may find himself before the easel of an idealist, a painter who conceives it to be his duty to make the most of the terrified person staring at him. Such a man will have the gift of putting the sitter at his ease, after which he may pursue the pleasant task of recording him as he would like to be. In this way the artist comes into coöperation with the Creator himself and softens or corrects His handiwork. No one has expressed this function of the merciful portraitist more aptly than Tennyson:

> As when a painter, poring on a face,
> Divinely thro' all hindrance finds the man
> Behind it, and so paints him that his face,
> The shape and colour of a mind and life,
> Lives for his children, ever at its best
> And fullest; so the face before her lived,
> Dark-splendid, speaking in the silence, full
> Of noble things.

I never see one of Romney's portraits of a man without thinking of these lines; for the artist has, as it were, looked with the eye of God, "divinely thro' all hindrance," and painted the sitter as he was meant to be. None surpassed Romney as a painter of boys, for he set them down on canvas in all the glowing promise of early youth. Thus his portrait of Lord Henry Petty, painted in the boy's eighth year, is an old bachelor's dream (in a happy moment) of what a son of his might have been.

Ideally, of course, a painter may become deeply indebted to his sitter, who may stir his imagination and send it out upon the wing. The result of this flight will be something other than the mere likeness of a model. Call it a fancy picture if you will: it is at least a subject that has released him from the drudgery of reproduction—the dull, difficult, and ignoble task of "face-painting"—and has enabled him to *create;* that is, to give local habitation and a name to the figures that haunt his dreams, since

from these create he can
Forms more real than living man.

As a spur to the imagination the best sitters are children, actors, and courtesans—persons, that is, who are free from the restrictions and neutralizing conventions of society. Think what the painters through all time have owed to their mistresses! To George Romney, Emma Lyon (afterward Lady Hamilton) was more than a mistress (if indeed she was ever that). To him she was alternately a Bacchante, a Cassandra, a nun in an ecstasy, Ariadne (or Contemplation), Medusa, a young girl reading the morning paper, and what not. David Garrick was a never failing inspiration to Reynolds and other painters, for he was no man, but Proteus, changing his expression and, let us add, his personality at will. He was that ideal sitter who co-operates with the artist in forwarding the work.

Children, actors, and courtesans, I say, for they are all compounded of pride and eager at any moment to exhibit themselves. They are without the *mauvaise honte* that makes a person hateful to himself and repellent to the painter. These happy beings delight in dressing up and pretending, for an intoxicating moment, to be something that they are not. Thus Reynolds surpassed himself when he painted Master Crewe (at the age of five?) as King Henry VIII, and Mrs. Siddons as the Tragic Muse.

Strange to relate, Sam Johnson, who was neither child nor actor, had this stimulating effect upon Reynolds, who painted him again and again, and on one occasion even depicted him as an infant Samuel. It must at some time have occurred to Sir Joshua to wonder how Johnson had looked at the age of two.

The vision came, and he painted the Doctor as a baby seated on the ground, with his head sunk in profound meditation on the insoluble problem of existence. At another time he painted Johnson as he fancied he must have appeared in his young manhood (long before the artist had ever seen him) as an aspirant in the literary world. He holds a copy of *Irene* in his hands, and rests his chin upon it.

He appears yet again in a purely imaginary role in that huge canvas which the President of the Royal Academy painted for Catherine of Russia, where he serves as a model for the figure of Tiresias (with the addition of a beard) in the lower left-hand corner of an allegorical scene. It is the "Infancy of Hercules," where the baby (Russia) is depicted as crushing the serpents in his cradle, and Tiresias is present as prophesying the future glory of the empire.

Keen must be the pleasure in the life of a model. It must be fun to dress up—or undress—and play for a time at being heroic warrior or sportive nymph, and there is no doubt that this childish pleasure has left its important mark upon portraiture. Courtiers, like children and actors, once delighted in it, as the popularity of the court masque and the *ballo in maschera* may serve to show. In such courtly amusements ladies and gentlemen found an opportunity to make themselves up as gods and goddesses and other desirable incarnations. The popularity and success of such entertainments afforded a stimulus to the painter, and the works of the Venetian and Parisian artists may be laid under contribution for examples.

I recall a portrait by Nattier in the Louvre in which the Duc de Chaulnes, with a wicked-looking club for a weapon and in the scanty attire of a lionskin, is represented as Hercules. It is all very surprising, if not absurd, till one realizes the significance of the subject as varying the tiresome routine of court portraiture and affording the artist a respite.

A painter will interest himself in anything to escape from the weary inspection of the countenance before him, which he has been hired to perpetuate on canvas. The temptation becomes acute when he is painting a portrait *en plein air,* for the landscape may well interest him more than the person in it, as is so often the case in the great landscape portraits of Gainsborough. He will even find relief in painting fabrics, as do the Dutch painters Vermeer, Dou, Terborch, and the rest. In Romney's portrait of Lady de la Pole (in Governor Fuller's collection) the seven folds of satin in her startling dress were said by contemporary opinion to be "more precious than any other folds of satin in the world." Vermeer's delight in a Persian rug or a nail-studded chair testifies to the universal Dutch delight in still life, in flowers, and in fish and vegetables and even the half-carved blushing ham.

A portrait painter is, by his very subject, limited to the depiction of the lesser passions and to such emotions as may safely be exhibited to the public. Since he can seldom hope to have a sitter of heroic spiritual stature, he is cut off from the sublime. Not for him is the legendary or epic grandeur of battle and tragedy; he cannot show the triumphant ecstasy of the saint, the spiritual corruption of a once noble character, the glory of the martyr, or the fall of the tyrant. Death and transfiguration are beyond his sphere. At best, he may but seize and perpetuate the momentary as did Hogarth—once and once only—in his picture of the Shrimp-seller.

What interests us in portraits is the skill of the painter, not the charm or vigor of the ladies or gentlemen who have the ridiculous notion that they somehow *are* the picture. Sir Thomas Lawrence painted a glorious portrait of Pope Pius VII (at Windsor Castle), and Van Dyck a yet more glorious one of King Charles I (in the Louvre), but the spectator will find as he dwells upon the likeness that his interest passes from pope or king to the artist with his "seeing eye." It is for the sitter, who must for one reason or another get himself painted, to pose a problem or issue a challenge to the painter, who will be a great fool if he is betrayed into producing merely a "speaking likeness."

I remember having been told an anecdote about Rodin, who had accepted a commission to carve a statue of the President of a South American republic. Since the completed figure was by no means a good likeness, the marble did not give satisfaction to the committee, who protested, *"Mais ce n'est pas notre Président,"* to which the sculptor is said to have retorted, *"Je l'ai vu comme ça."* I cannot vouch for the historicity of this incident; but, even if false, it embodies the principle that in all portraiture the important thing is that which the artist sees.

Of what *lasting* importance is the sitter's satisfaction or that of his friends and admirers (if he has any) with their insistent demand for a likeness? In fifty years, of what account will the most accurate likeness be? Who will care for the mere resemblance when the person shown is already dust and ashes? The only matter of importance then will be what the painter found, or detected as of more than passing significance in the sitter before him.

And so in those audacious creatures who sit for their picture a certain humility is becoming. The painter will be remembered and praised for his divine skill; the sitter will be forgotten or faded into a mere historical document. A merciful oblivion may reduce the proud beauty to nothing more than an anonymous entry in some future catalogue, "Portrait of a Lady," while what the artist was at pains to learn about us and took his precious time to tell—this will endure. The glowing eulogy, the stinging satire, will live on, and it is thus that the artist shall at last prevail, and triumph over the employer who hired him.

XIV

The Quality of Mercy

An Address delivered before the Graduating Class of the School of Nursing of the Presbyterian Hospital. 1929.

IN the pleasant town of Pistoja, not many miles from Florence, there stands what must certainly be one of the most beautiful hospitals in the world, the Ospedale del Ceppo. To our American way of thought it seems small, almost tiny, for it is only two stories high, and hopelessly antiquated; it was built in the early sixteenth century. It is of the most exquisite proportions, with a beautiful loggia, consisting of seven round arches, extending across the entire front of the building and forming a long, high veranda. On the gray wall, above the arches, there lies, like a band of opalescent light, a broad border of colored sculpture in high relief, as bright as a garden of flowers. This long frieze, with figures and scenes in glazed terracotta, is believed to be the work of Giovanni Della Robbia and the two Buglioni. United with it and symbolic of the whole building are allegorical figures of Charity and certain other virtues. The climate, mercifully dry, has preserved the seven panels which form that border, as they could never have been preserved on the exterior of any northern building. Moreover, the comparative lowness of the colonnade brings them sufficiently near to the eye of a person in the square below so that he can distinguish details, and follow the general subject as it develops from left to right, like a series of illustrations.

As one comes gradually to grasp the details, one is disconcerted by the painful and even repulsive nature of the scenes before him, as the artists have chosen to illustrate the extremes of human misery. Here are naked wretches, starving beggars, footsore wayfarers, sick folk and dying folk, ulcers, dirt, disease, and corpses. These are realistic pictures of the life of the poor at the close of the Middle Ages, and, for a reason that we shall understand presently, there has been no attempt to soften the harshness of the scenes. One of these panels is an important document in the history of medicine, since it shows the interior of a hospital of the early sixteenth century. The patients are lying in beds, duly numbered. What patient ever went unnumbered? It is a busy scene. On one side a surgeon is dressing a scalp wound, while the patient, supported by a nurse, grasps the doctor's forearm in an agony, and with the other hand convulsively clutches the bedding. Opposite, a physician, with bowed head and fixed gaze, is taking a patient's pulse. The nursing brothers-in-charge are assisted by various attendants, some making records in a notebook, others bearing in food or basins of water. When we reflect that we are separated from this life by over four hundred years, it is a startling bit of realism, as though one had opened a window, and suddenly looked out into another world. And then one pulls himself up with a start, and remembers that it is all part of a piece of architectural decoration.

One wonders what an ancient Greek sculptor, accustomed to the representation of graceful goddesses, splendid athletes, and heroic warriors would think of ornamentation such as this, with its emphasis on human misery, dirt, and need. It would be necessary, I suppose, to point out to such a one that the emphasis is, after all, not so much on misery as on the relief of it. If the figures in the panels are hungry, they are being fed, if naked, they are being clothed, if sick, they are being healed, and so on. The very name which is properly applied to the whole series of seven panels reveals this fact. These pictures represent the medieval system of charity—the "organized relief" of the sixteenth century. By the Church these various sorts of charity were known as Corporal Works of Mercy, because they were meant for the relief of the body. It is mercy that is glorified, and not misery. The subjects were chosen by the brotherhood who had erected the hospital, in order to touch the hearts of beholders and move them to support the charitable work of the foundation. In the same way, on the Foundling Hospital in Florence, the Della Robbias had been commissioned to sculpture the figures of babies in swaddling clothes, which form a series of lovely medallions in blue and white across the façade of that building.

Everybody in the sixteenth century who glanced up at the pictures on the façade of the Hospital recognized the subjects at once, as we should recognize, let us say, the four seasons sculptured on a courthouse. They had heard of the Seven Works of Mercy before, and they knew from these pictures that the Order or "foundation" that erected the house consisted of Brothers of Mercy, who had dedicated their lives to practical Christianity, with its specific duties of (1) feeding the hungry; (2) giving drink to the thirsty; (3) clothing the naked; (4) relieving prisoners; (5) sheltering travelers; (6) nursing the sick; and (7) burying the dead. This particular division of charitable duties goes back to the words of Christ in St. Matthew's Gospel: "For I was an hungered, and ye gave me meat: I was thirsty, and ye gave me drink. I was a stranger, and ye took me in: Naked and ye clothed me: I was sick and ye visited me. I was in prison, and ye came unto me." Here are six of the "works" of which I have been speaking, lacking only the burial of the dead to bring them up to the familiar seven.

Over them, medieval theology pored with loving attention, until these seven forms of suffering and their relief seemed to open out and embrace all charitable enterprise of a practical kind.

But, you will be protesting, there are other forms of charity beside these—schools, for instance. To be sure; but these were provided for in another category. For if there are seven corporal works of mercy, there are seven spiritual ones also. They are closely related to the corporal works, however; and the two groups together constitute a fourteenfold category of duties to oneself and one's neighbors. These spiritual works are: (1) to instruct the ignorant; (2) to correct offenders; (3) to counsel the doubtful; (4) to comfort the afflicted; (5) to bear injuries patiently; (6) to forgive offenders; and (7) to pray for the living and the dead.

You will see at once that there is a subtle connection between the two sets. There is a similarity, for instance, between caring for the sick and comforting the afflicted; between feeding the body and storing the mind. Nurse and professor, according to such a philosophy, are pretty much alike. The medieval mind delighted in discovering and elaborating such relationships as these because they enforced the great truth that all healing of the body implied a healing of the spirit. Do you recall the words of Macbeth to the doctor who has failed in his ministration to Lady Macbeth?

> Canst thou not minister to a mind diseased,
> Pluck from the memory a rooted sorrow,
> Raze out the written troubles of the brain,

And with some sweet oblivious antidote
Cleanse the stuff'd bosom of that perilous stuff
Which weighs upon the heart?

They could see plainly enough, those students of the corporal works of mercy, that what gives force and validity to charity is the merciful attitude of mind.

It is a fatally easy thing to lose. As soon as any charitable work develops into a *system,* the life tends to go out of it. When we are ministering to the body, it is painfully easy to forget the poor, suffering person within. He is, with great appropriateness sometimes, called a *patient;* for he must learn to bear injuries with patience. I vividly recall an illustration of this truth that system hardens the heart, and though a trivial anecdote it illustrates my purpose so admirably, that I shall brave your contempt by telling it. In 1917 when drafted men were being examined for the service, it was, at one time, my humble office to act as a dentist's assistant. The men appeared before the dental examiners in line, an endless, naked line, like a vast flesh-colored reel of tape, extending across one side of the room, down another, and at last out of a door into a hall beyond—unbroken, continuous. As the dental surgeon examined the victims, he would call out, "Extract lower five," "Extract upper eight," and similar directions, which I entered upon cards. The miserable being, having listened to his fate with such composure as he could muster while his teeth were, so to speak, being voted away from him—and all by way of driving back the Germans some thousands of miles away—was then dismissed with a word of personal direction from the dentist's assistant, myself, as to the course which he must, dentally speaking, pursue. At first, I recall, I was vividly aware of the human being before me whose emotions regarding the removal of "lower five" and "upper eight" were necessarily different from mine; but by the time I had repeated my directions to a hundred, my patients were no more to me than so many cattle. I might as well have been a slave driver. I should have had no uneasy feelings in seeing them chucked aboard a transport with as much tenderness as a baggage smasher shows for a steamer trunk.

The human soul is a fearful thing when the quality of mercy has gone out of it. Well may a patient pray to be delivered from a nurse who is so scientifically trained and so perfectly equipped as to be past all feeling.

And this hardheartedness is sure to descend upon us when we put our whole trust in science and the "system," to the total exclusion of feeling. It is easy to treat a patient as though he were a felon, an offender against that sacred law of modern life which bids us be perpetually rosy and beaming disciples of progress, full of 100 per cent corn-fed efficiency. It is easy to think of a sick person as a bale of damaged goods consigned to the tomb, a cadaverous object that ought to be thankful for any treatment he gets from the exponents of science, to whom as a patient he may be useful for purposes of demonstration.

This temptation to treat disease as a crime is amusingly set forth in a very readable book by Samuel Butler, called *Erewhon*. Erewhon—the spelling is an anagram of "nowhere," Utopia— is an imaginary country in which all the people are healthy and prosperous, and into which a person from our world wanders by mistake. He discovers, to his astonishment, that in this topsy-turvy land, crime is regarded exactly as we regard disease. A person there will refer to his temptations to steal or embezzle or murder with the same freedom which we use in talking of a cold in the head or a fit of rheumatism. When he feels an attack coming on, he puts himself at once into the hands of a specialist who prescribes a course of treatment designed to correct the failing. While the attack lasts he is the subject of condolences from his friends, who comfort him with accounts of similar disorders of their own, and, if he recovers, all congratulate him and join in trusting that the malady will not recur.

The true criminal in this ideal land is the sick man.

In that country if a man falls into ill health, or catches any disorder, or fails bodily in any way before he is seventy years old, he is tried before a jury of his countrymen, and if convicted, is held up to public scorn and sentenced more or less severely as the case may be. There are subdivisions of illnesses into crimes and misdemeanors as with offenses among ourselves.

Duing his visit to this country, the narrator is present at the trial of a young man charged with suffering from tuberculosis.
The sentence was as follows:

Prisoner at the bar, you have been accused of the great crime of laboring under pulmonary consumption, and after an impartial trial before a jury of your countrymen, you have been found guilty. Against the justice of the verdict I can say nothing: the evidence against you was conclusive, and it only remains for me to pass such sentence upon you, as shall satisfy the ends of the law. That sentence must be a very severe one. It pains me much to see one who is yet so young, and whose prospects in life were otherwise so excellent, brought to this distressing condition by a constitution which I can only regard as radically vicious; but yours is no case for compassion: this is not your first offense: you have led a career of crime, and have only profited by the leniency shown you upon past occasions, to offend yet more seriously against the laws and institutions of your country. You were convicted of aggravated bronchitis last year: and I find that though you are now only twenty-three years old, you have been imprisoned on no less than fourteen occasions for illnesses of more or less hateful character; in fact, it is not too much to say that you have spent the greater part of your life in a jail.

It is all very well for you to say that you came of unhealthy parents, and had a severe accident in your childhood which permanently undermined your constitution; excuses such as these are the ordinary refuge of the criminal; but they cannot for one moment be listened to by the ear of justice. I am not here to enter upon curious metaphysical questions as to the origin of this or that—questions as to which there would be no end were their introduction once tolerated, and which would result in throwing the only guilt on the tissues of the primordial cell, or on the elementary gases. There is no question of how you came to be wicked, but only this—namely, are you wicked or not?

Needless to say the prisoner is condemned. The sentence is hard labor for what remains of his miserable existence.

Hospitals, even in these altered times, with all their new and marvelous equipment, cannot be unconcerned with the corporal works of mercy, however aptly they be renamed; and nurses and patients alike will be the happier according as they reflect on this great truth. I think I have the makings of a very good patient in me. I am, for example, by nature, obedient and even submissive, if I know what my duty is; and I am constrained to say that I have never met a nurse who was not quite ready to make that duty clear to me. I love to lie still in bed and have things done for me. If to these blessings can be added the cheerful boon of silence, my cup of contentment is full. I am repaid for the loss of my treasured privacy. I can die or recover in peace.

You who are accustomed to listening to sermons will realize

that I am speaking, even though playfully, of the two great unpopular virtues of obedience and humility. Fine, old-fashioned, drab-colored virtues, out of which, like a butterfly from the chrysalis, arose most of the color and beauty of life. Fine old-fashioned virtues, I say, which were known to that simple brotherhood in Pistoja four centuries ago; and known also, let me add, to the artist who, seeing the beauty of their life, carved the lovely representation of it on the walls of their house. For what artist ever mastered the technique of sculpture without discipline as hard as any nurse's, and what is discipline but obedience? The men that carved and painted that glowing panel had learned to submit; they had learned to subordinate personality to the art in which they worked, content to disappear behind it if only beauty might issue out of it.

One might build up a whole theory of art on that relation between the life of the hospital and the sculpture that adorns its walls: the color and glory of the carving which arises out of the life in progress within the building; and that life, in its turn, made possible by the poverty, obedience and humility to which the brotherhood was dedicated. It is always so. Some principle is discovered to which it seems worth while to sacrifice life—I mean the casual, undirected life about us; then a new life gathers round it as its fitting embodiment; and last of all, when it has reached its fullness of beauty, it inspires the artist who perpetuates it in its splendor.

XV

Ancestor Worship

WITH SOME REMARKS ABOUT THE SEA WORM

IT would be mere affection in writing about ancestors to avoid all personal references and pretend to be indifferent to one's own. There is nothing for it but to speak out. It is comforting to reflect, however, that one cannot be personal very long; for if you go any distance backward in your analysis you presently lose yourself in a crowd that is unflatteringly promiscuous. If you ascend as far as the twentieth generation in tracing your lineage, mathematics will tell you—doubtless quite erroneously—that you have already something over a million ancestors in all, and though there are subtractions to be made from this appalling number by reason of the crossing and recrossing of the lines of descent, the number remains large. In any case, it will be too large for an inclusive view.

There are people all about us who coolly select from the mob those individuals from whom it satisfies their vanity to be descended, so that in a sense they are selecting their own ancestry. Even among our four grandparents most of us had our favorite. Proximity or the mere fact of their survival made us better acquainted with one than with the rest; and no doubt it was better so, for a superfluity of grandparents might prove embarrassing to a child. And if, to pile Ossa on Pelion, you enter upon the next stage and contemplate the atavistic complexities of your eight great-grandparents, the problem begins to take on something of the mystery and majesty that mark all profound matters. I once met a man who could remember, beside his four grandparents, three of his great-grandparents. The sum of his ancestors—parents, grandparents, and great-grandparents—with whom he had come into something like personal contact—whom he had at least seen—was therefore nine, a number of bonds with the past which would, I fear, have proved disturbing to my sense of individuality.

I myself was not so blessed. There was nothing—indeed, there never has been anything—to prevent me from conceiving of myself quite as individualistically as I choose. My paternal grandmother was the only one of my grandparents with whom I was acquainted, a lovable but stern Puritan lady from the Connecticut Valley, who had read Fox's *Book of Martyrs,* and was said to have sheltered a runaway slave girl. Our ancestors, as I came to know them through her, were a sufficiently uninteresting group, farmers in Connecticut, who, like so many others there, seem never to have done very well. The only thing that appears to have distinguished our farm from the score of sterile estates that environed it was a cranberry bog, a sufficiently uncertain foundation on which to build any family pride.

A vague rumor which I once heard, and which seemed singularly inappropriate to such an ordinary family as ours, had it that one of our ancestors had been hanged as a pirate in the Bahamas. I have the most serious doubts about the historicity of this legend, though it is almost as gratifying to have a family pirate as it is to have a family ghost, and I suspect some primitive genealogist of trying thus to lend a tang of romance to an otherwise drab tradition. If he really existed, the buccaneer bequeathed nothing of his adventurous disposition to me, for I do not recollect that I ever longed to be a pirate. I am aware that heroic little boys ought to want to grow up to be pirates, but I was by no means an heroic little boy. My great ambition was to be a conductor on the Boston & Maine railway. And even this besetting desire I should have difficulty in accounting for on any theory of heredity. We were not a race of travelers or gadabouts, unless the family name be taken to connect us with those wayfarers who moved up and down the roads and lanes of England mending pots and pans, lending, meanwhile, force and color to the English vocabulary.

There was a fine paternalism about the old Boston & Maine. The conductor, it seems, always shook hands with one's father, and sometimes—oh, bliss—bestowed a salutation (from Olympus) on the small boy at his side. At a certain point in the journey, a brakeman dispensed ice water from a copper teakettle, and at the end the blue and gold conductor, having collected all his pink slips, dismissed you with a warning cry not to forget your "packages, wraps, and umbrellas." Yes, that was the life for a man! Journeying about the world, armed with a small and fascinating device for punching holes in tickets, bestowing smiles and warning cries—obviously the god of that particular machine. In all my clerical and agricultural ancestry I had heard of none so glorious as he. In my wild desire to be a conductor there could have been no atavism, no snapback toward the past. It was the soul's leap toward the glorious and the impossible, the desire of the moth for the star.

Even if we had been a race of conductors, I am not sure that I should have been permitted to take any pride in my relationship to them, since no particular respect for ancestors was inculcated in the young of our family. There was no hint that we need be ashamed of our forebears, whatever the truth might be about that dark soul who had perished in the Bahamas. But in the stout old days before the New Englanders had moved out to make room for the Italians, children were not encouraged to take pride in such vanities. At the very best, one's line ended in Adam and Eve, whose deplorable conduct was a perpetual reminder of an innate perverseness of heart in human beings, and particularly in little boys. Not that we were permitted to deride or denounce poor Adam and Eve. No, indeed. Had we been in their position, our teachers urged us to consider, how deplorably similar, how much worse in all likelihood, *our* conduct would have been. If Adam and Eve were punished for a trifle, in a new and beautiful world, what pray were naughty boys to expect, who disobeyed, and didn't love their fellowmen or, mayhap, ran away to become conductors on the Boston & Maine? It was the traditional attitude of the Puritan, the ancient argument, and I am glad to have heard it, not only for its inherent truthfulness, but for the views that it opened up to me. "Dost thou hear, Hal?" said Falstaff. "Thou knowest in the state of innocency Adam fell, and what should poor Jack Falstaff do in the days of villainy?"

In our modern, scientifically trained generation it has become difficult for some persons to read the story of our first parents understandingly. We have become so imbued with the conception of progress that we tend even to read the fall of man as a sort of majestic catastrophe that made progress possible.

Better the mad yearning and tragedy of growth through imperfection than the serene stagnation of the ideal. This view is brilliantly expressed by Mr. Neil Grant, who utters this surprising theory: "There is something extraordinarily uplifting in the thought that man, once the equal of angels, had the courage and the will to fall down to his present level."

What is all this about man having once been the equal of the angels, and having had the initiative and resolution to fall? Has Mr. Grant never read Milton, not to speak of the Holy Bible? Certainly he could not have had the luck to be born in old New England in the days when children knew Adam and Eve as well as a modern youngster knows an ichthyosaurus. As though man had had any choice as to whether to fall gloriously or go on being perfect. Man's fall was due to a cantankerous and unlovely desire to have his own way, and there is nothing "uplifting" about it. It may have been fun but it certainly was not courageous. And what does any of us know about the state of the angels from which man had this curious will to depart? But Mr. Grant, being modern, doesn't really believe in angels any more than he does in snarks. So what difference does it make if his snark turns out to be a boojum anyhow?

It would certainly have seemed odd to any Puritan to take a special pride in a descent from Adam and Eve (even if they were the equal of the angels) odd and probably sinful. But to take pride in man's descent from animals has become a habit among the modern disciples of evolution, and has indeed the august authority of the discoverer of the origin of species. In a famous passage at the very close of *The Descent of Man*, Darwin wrote,

Man may be excused for feeling some pride at having risen, though not through his own exertions, to the very summit of the organic scale, and the fact of his having thus risen, instead of having been aboriginally placed there, may give him hope for a still higher destiny in the distant future.

Well, here is more cause for pride. If we take pride (with Mr. Grant) in our fall, we may also take pride (with Darwin) in our rise to the summit of the organic scale, though what good it does us to be there is perhaps a question to be asked. But much pseudoscientific nonsense issued out of this emotion of Darwin's. Drummond's *Ascent of Man,* a book now forgotten, expanded this Darwinian view of things, and taught us to take pride in the upward trend of man's development. But to me it all seems sadly remote. Who can care very much about what happened so long ago? I accept, cordially enough of course, the whole evolutionary hypothesis; but what has *pride* to do with it? Pride and humiliation seem out of place in the study of science as in history. I read about the Punic wars—or did at one time—with a certain detachment, and the remote history of the race, in its simian and pithecanthropic stages leaves my emotions untouched. I cannot glow with gratitude at the names of Piltdown and Neanderthal. It is all so dreadfully long ago. And at this rate where is one to end? We shall soon be asked to take pride in the primitive division of the amoebic cell.

Yet Darwin did not hesitate to express his emotions about it all. The most famous sentences in his famous book were perhaps these, in which he would seem to be offering some consolation to the world that he was accused of having humiliated.

For my own part I would as soon be descended from that heroic little monkey who braved his dreaded enemy in order to save the life of his keeper, or from that old baboon who, descending from the mountains, carried away in triumph his young comrade from a crowd of astonished dogs, as from a savage who delights to torture his enemies, offers up bloody sacrifices, practises infanticide without remorse, treats his wives like slaves, knows no decency, and is haunted by the grossest superstitions.

Here surely is an appeal to the emotions which a modern scientist must deplore. What have heroic monkeys and affectionate baboons or bloodthirsty and superstitious savages to do with it all, save to prepare the way for Mowgli and Tarzan and other fine reversions to type? How much pure Jack Londonism there is in this attitudinizing of Darwin's. The great scientist writes as if he were permitted to *choose* whether he would be descended from a savage or a baboon, whereas the plain truth, which even a literary man may see, is that he is, willy-nilly, descended from them both. He cannot get rid of the savage by allying himself with the baboons; he must take the disgrace of the head-hunter and the cannibal along with the glory of the chimpanzee.

Something of that bravado which found satisfaction in its descent from apes or apelike men, or Pithecanthropus erectus (or whatever the proper modern term for him may be) has passed away with the Huxleys and the Spencers, and the people that took pride in holding a new view of the universe. We are, as a whole, conscious of an ancestry humble indeed compared with the ape and the lemur. Mr. Grant may be taken as a fair example of that reader who has learned of his past from Mr. H. G. Wells and the anthropologists whom he in turn derives from. The idea, he says, is gradually soaking into the popular mind "that man, far from being once the equal of the angels, has developed painfully and slowly from the sea-worm, which one fine day was daring enough to leave the ocean for the land . . . How can we be hero-worshippers when we think of the sea-worm?"

Here is a new note, humility. Instead of taking pride in Darwin's heroic little monkey, I must now humbly recall the sea worm, who points me still further backward to the amoeba. Having confronted my imagination with a vast cloud of witnesses, extending in long line back to the very bubbles in the slime, I am to reflect on my extraction from the mud and be humble. But if Darwin could be proud of monkey and baboon, why may I not be proud remembering the adventurous sea worm and all the plucky little vermin from whom I am descended, and whom I so obviously resemble?

In answering this somewhat rhetorical question, we must notice first that it is much harder to visualize a sea worm than a monkey. Every child delights in monkeys but (I suppose) only the children of biologists have a bowing acquaintance with sea worms. Darwin, moreover, however sentimental he may have been, did what all ancestor worshipers do—he selected those from whom he was willing to be descended and ignored the rest. Whether he was conscious of it or not, he fixed his attention on an individual monkey and an individual baboon as proper heroes to be descended from, whereas Mr. Wells and the modern anthropologists performed the far more difficult task of remembering them in the mass. Mr. Grant does this in the interest of humility and as an opponent of hero worship. But the task, even for those who have imagination enough to succeed in it, is unpalatable. Men in the mass are not admirable. Men and their ancestors through myriads of centuries, viewed in the mass, are loathsome, not because they are monkeys or worms or reptiles, but just because they are so numerous. Nothing sickens the heart like numbers.

If you ascend to the roof of a New York skyscraper and look down upon your kind in the busy street below, you will there see men as maggots. You cannot look into their eyes and divine the farce or the tragedy that is being enacted within their spirit; therefore you see them as tiny, racing mites, appearing in the mass impersonal, galvanized, antlike.

If you wish to love an animal, you must separate it from its kind, even if it be a lamb. Restore your creature to the pack, and out goes the affection between you. You cannot love a swarm of bees, even if you are an idiot. No one except M. Maeterlinck, I suppose, ever tried to, and he, quite characteristically, selected the queen bee as the object of his more ardent attention.

When I was a boy I was interested in ants, and, following biblical precept, spent some time in their contemplation. I grew fond of ants, in a way, and came to know something of their habits; but it was once my misfortune to be with a whole army of them. From that time onward, my whole attitude toward the industrious race suffered a change. Ants, thousands and thousands of them, swarmed about me, and I was both mortified and afraid. There were ants on my hands and in my face; in my shoes ants were concealed; they appeared in every part of my clothing, while hordes of reënforcements came from nowhere, and when at last I emerged from the unequal conflict, it was with a fear of pismires that would, no doubt, appear contemptible to those unaware of the experience I had had.

Well, I have no desire to deluge my imagination in any such way with the incalculable myriads of my ancestors. The globe on which we exist would have no more dignity for me than a crawling cheese.

I repeat that what depresses one in the story of evolution is the promiscuous feature of it, the necessity of regarding the world as a vast breeding and hatching ground, swarming with crawling creatures, sucking, snarling, breeding, dying things, devoured by more crawling creatures, bloody-fanged, who suck and snarl and breed and die.

It is not safe to think in this wise. But there is nothing unpleasant, as any child or any savage will tell you, about conceiving yourself as blood brother to the animals. It has never been deemed a disgrace to call a man a lion or a girl a gazelle. Many persons say that they prefer the society of their dog to that of most human beings.

Pass to the less noble animals, and still the relationship is so close that it cannot be denied, and nobody blushes for it. When I visit the zoo, I renew my acquaintance with my friends and associates and admit my descent from the animals. I look into my heart and there I find the pig and the peacock struggling for preëminence.

In all this there is much that results from early training, for I was always taught that man was an animal. Even in the same breath that I was taught to believe myself the child of God and heir of eternal life, I was reminded that I was but dust, and that to dust I was destined to return. Is the mud of the biologist any more mortifying than the clay and dust of the prophets?

Pride, humility, and attendant emotions are all proportionate to the perspective in which the world is viewed. It is all a matter of proportion, sea worm or heroic monkey, conductor on the Boston & Maine or angel in glory—destroy the perspective in which they are viewed, and the emotions with which they are regarded change or disappear. Of what conceivable importance is the whole evolutionary drama if you remove yourself to a sufficient distance from it? There is an advertisement in the popular magazines which shows a clock dial beside the countenance of a primitive man and invites the reader to reflect that if the entire career of the human race be estimated as occupying the twelve hours marked on the dial, then it may be said that man has so far lived, as it were, but a minute and a quarter, according to such reckoning of time.

Perhaps the implication of this emblem is that there is plenty of time yet for man to achieve that perfection and complete that progress which have seemed to be so seriously threatened during the past decade. But I cannot, when once this hideous conception of time has entered my mind, take any comfort in the eleven hours and fifty-eight minutes that remain. For imagine a lapse of time, say of three months to be counted off on that dreadful clock; take, if you can, such a giddy plunge into the abyss of eternity, and then look back and ask what conceivable significance those twelve hours had. What meaning was there in the whole history of the human race, the whole evolutionary process or even the history of the planet itself from its inception in fire to its death in ice? A bubble bursting in the endless night of time. This way, too, lies madness, and there is no cure for the vertiginous sickness which it begets save to turn to the nearest human being and think of a mystery less benumbing.

There is a vast fallacy in all this inquiry into origins, since it rests upon the false assumption that the history of a phenomenon is its explanation. When the biologists have completed their researches, and the whole history of man is known from the first flicker of consciousness down to the full emergence of *Homo sapiens,* the explanation of it all will still elude us. *Causa latet.*

Suppose that the whole history of man could be compressed into a moving picture, and in some dreadful "educational film" you could watch the development on the screen of man from the sea worm to Socrates, just as we now watch the development of a plant, would the mystery be any less of a mystery?

In other ages the problem of man's relation to animals was stated in a different and perhaps a more illuminating way. Man, it was said, is an animal, a biped without feathers. He is an animal that wears clothes or some other odd covering for ornament if not for warmth; he is not satisfied with the skin and hair provided for him, but prefers another pattern. The strange creature takes pride in the thing that he winds round himself.

Again, man is an animal that uses tools. One of the famous assaults on the dignity of man in the eighteenth century consisted of an attempt to show that the *orangutan* used a stick as a weapon, and engravings were published—notably in Goldsmith's *History of Animated Nature,* showing the beast thus armed and standing in front of rude huts that he had built for his shelter.

Man is the animal that writes, draws, and records his invisible thoughts in tangible form, thus initiating civilization as we know it. He is the animal that speaks, the animal that laughs. These differences make up a sum so astonishing that they seem to demonstrate that man is something other than, or something in addition to, an animal. The mad creature desires to change everything, himself included. Unlike a dog or a bee or an ape, he is either fretting about himself or dreaming about himself, vexed by his desire to get something out of reach. For which reason he, the most gregarious of beasts, slew his fellows, and took from them, and remained unsatisfied. In his dreams about himself, he fabled that he was not wholly of this world, but that he came from afar and was, indeed, the child of the sun or the remote descendant of a god, prince in his own right. A mad creature indeed. He was not ashamed of his kinship with animals and even courted a likeness to them; but unlike them, he looked forward to a good time ahead, whether it was to consist of stealing a number of women from a neighboring tribe, or passing at last to a heavenly mansion prepared in advance for one so important as himself. What if this be midsummer madness, lunacy of the plainest sort? It must still be explained. You cannot get rid of a problem by calling it mad.

The conclusion from these reflections on the general nature of man, in days before thinkers were obsessed by the mere history of the race, was that man must be two different but strangely related things, inseparably connected, yet destined one day to be dissolved. Man was *pulvis et umbra,* a shadow of the eternal cast upon the dust, a spark of fire, caught in a clod. To fix your attention on one of these to the exclusion of the other is to throw everything out of proportion, and in reality to give up the problem, for the paradox is at its very heart. A clod, to be sure, with a history; an animal to be sure, with ancestors, but an animal conducting itself in a preposterous way, a divine-infernal way that, apart from man, is surely not of this world. For which reason such thinkers habitually taught that man was an animal, or rather all sorts of animal at once, an ass in sloth, a wolf in wrath, a goat in lust, a hog in gluttony; indeed they taught that he was beneath all these because he had within him a standard of conduct that was of a different order of life altogether, and to which he had been disloyal. This was the spiritual part of him, and its origin was confidently explained as being in another sphere, beyond present comprehension. Dust shall return to dust, and the spirit shall go to its own place. "Magnificent out of the dust we came, and abject from the spheres."

Because of this high origin, and yet higher destiny, it was deemed wise not to dwell too long upon our ancestors in this world, for to do so is to obscure the problem which is man. You are yourself the problem; you are the theater of a struggle between two powers for the possession of your soul, and it is the issue of the struggle, not its origin, which is of the greater importance. All that we know of the absorption of interest in genealogy enforces the same truth. If a man is largely interested in the social position of his grandmother, it usually militates against his humanity and his charity. It is a terrible thing to be, like a king, the victim of your ancestors, never to escape from the iron cage in which your descent has imprisoned you. If you find yourself in bonds, like a duke or a drunkard, you may, I doubt not, take a dubious satisfaction in tracing your faulty character to your forebears. But for the vast multitude of my own, dear human souls unknown to me even by name, I will take leave of them all with a flourish of salutation, as did Charles Surface in the play, after he had sold his ancestors to the highest bidder: "Ladies and gentlemen, your most obedient and very grateful servant." I wave a calm and I hope graceful farewell to them across the vista of the years. I wish them well and, for that matter, rest eternal. And in this gesture of farewell, I should like to include in the wide sweep of my ceremonious bow, the ape, the lemur, and—well, yes—even the sea worm.

INDEX

ADDISON, JOSEPH, his *Letter from Italy,* quoted by Johnson, 26; prose style praised by Johnson, 31

Altschul, Frank, his catalogue of a Meredith Collection, 83

Ancestors, worship of, 144 ff.

Arnold, Matthew, characterization of Shelley, 43

Arts, elusiveness of today, 123; need of, 125

Auden, W. H., mentioned, 8, 98

BARLOW, JOEL, his *Vision of Columbus,* 37 ff.; mentions colleges (Harvard, Yale, and Princeton), cotton, lightning rod, and tobacco plant, 41–42

Beerbohm, Sir Max, *Rossetti and His Circle,* 80–82

Boston & Maine Railroad, 146

Boswell, James, 16, 18

Brontë, Anne, poetry of, 53, 56, 57
—— Charlotte, poetry of, 56–59
—— Emily, poetry of, 55, 57–61

Buglioni, the, sculptors, work at Pistoja, 135

Burney, Frances (Mme. D'Arblay), 18

Butler, Samuel, his *Erewhon,* 141

CHARITY, sixteenth century, 136 ff.

Chaulnes, Duc de, painted as "Hercules," 131

Coorte, Adrian, 120

Courtiers, portraits of, in fancy dress, 131

Crane, Walter, 7

DARWIN, CHARLES, his *Descent of Man,* quoted, 149

Daudet, Alphonse, his *La Doulou,* 13

Dentist's assistant, author's experience as, 139

Diaries, nature of, 10 ff.

Drummond, the Reverend Henry, his *Ascent of Man,* 149

Dutch School of painting, charm of their still life, 120, 132

ELIOT, T. S., 8, 9

Empedocles, Meredith's poem on, 87

Evolution, doctrine of, as begetting pride? or humility? 148–150

FAIRFAX, EDWARD, translator of Tasso, 3

Fall of man, doctrine of, 147

Ferguson, DeLancey, 94

GOLDSMITH, OLIVER, 24, 155

Gosse, Sir Edmund, 52, 81

Grant, Dr. Neil, 150

HAZLITT, WILLIAM, 127 note

Hogarth, William, his "Shrimp Seller," 132

Horace, his tenth Epode, quoted, 94

Hospitals in the sixteenth century, 136

Housman, A. E., Professor, *A Shropshire Lad* (1896), 93; *Last Poems* (1922), 91; *The Name and Nature of Poetry* (1933), 99 ff.; Americans, attitude to, 100; Christianity, attitude, to, 97; disillusion, 95; "Epitaph on an Army of Mercenaries," quoted, 96; intelligible, 102; juvenilia, has no, 91; Kipling, resemblance to, in one poem, 95; "lad," fondness for the word, 92; middle